HR APPROVED WAYS TO SAY (ALMOST) ANYTHING TO COWORKERS

500+ TIPS ON HOW TO TALK TO ANYONE AT WORK & MASTER WORKPLACE COMMUNICATION WITH HUMOR, EVEN WITH DIFFICULT PEOPLE

S.R. BROWN

HALCYON ENTERPRISE INC.

CONTENTS

Paperback

ISBN: 979-8-9927679-1-9

PROLOGUE

When you come across those moments at work when your patience is about to snap, that's when you really start to see what some of your coworkers are truly like and when you begin to notice, shall we say, a range of smarts, some of which are definitely on the lower end.

That's where this book comes in, to help you deal with these situations without getting yourself fired. Think of this book as your guide to tricky coworker communication, when you really want to call a coworker an idiot. But you know, you can't.

INTRODUCTION

We've all been there, right? Wanting to just say what's on your mind to your colleagues, but you know, without getting fired. Think of this book as your secret weapon for those tough talks, it's the cheat code for having HR-approved conversations.

Now, this isn't about giving you the green light to just say whatever pops into your head. Even though, let's be real, that is tempting, it's more about being able to get your thoughts across while being mindful of workplace relationships. And of course, being aware that HR is always listening.

I still remember one time I was sitting at the desk across from our company's vice president during our weekly scheduled one-on-one. His concentration was intently on his email inbox. He was clearly preoccupied, and then abruptly asked, "Where's the meeting agenda?" He let out a sigh, adding, "Please, just always email it to me."

I was taken aback by his coarse tone and his unfounded assumptions. Calmly, I replied, "It's actually in the calendar notes. I always include bullet points about the meeting topics directly in the meeting invite."

"Oh," was all he could muster. He was visibly surprised. I couldn't resist gently adding, "Yeah, because do you really need another email?" We both burst out in laughter.

This short exchange isn't a one-time event—it's a performance played out in offices every day. It's the too-familiar convo that comes from battling inefficiency, miscommunication, and small aggravations that erode our patience and productivity. But in these exchanges lies a possibility: that of transforming annoyance into wisdom, frustration into humor, and confusion into insight.

We will navigate these too-familiar moments in the coming chapters, side by side, by extracting real-world strategies for turning onsite and remote workplace issues into drivers of growth, understanding, and constructive change. Welcome to the light-hearted, entertaining guidebook to surviving and thriving in everyday workplace life.

Wherever you work, it can sometimes resemble living in a bizarre sitcom—where meetings last an eternity, emails multiply like rabbits, and a coworker brags about less than helpful training about something you've known since forever. If you've ever endured an unnecessary meeting or bitten your tongue while a coworker breaks down the in-your-face obvious, you're reading the right book.

And now, let's address the "(Almost) Anything" in the title. The phrase "(Almost) Anything" refers to the wide range of sensitive, awkward, or difficult workplace topics that employees frequently encounter—but might hesitate to discuss openly or directly. It's important to keep in mind that "(Almost) Anything" is used here humorously, with a generous dose of satire and irony.

Far from being critical, think of it as gentle, tongue-in-cheek shorthand —a playful way to approach those sensitive workplace situations that can be tricky, or difficult to navigate. The purpose isn't to criticize coworkers harshly, but rather to highlight actions that go against common sense, all within a humorous and respectful framework.

When I refer to saying "(Almost) Anything," think of it as addressing workplace behavior that might otherwise seem uncomfortable, frustrating, or simply baffling. We're not speaking with coworkers negatively; instead, we're finding clever, HR-approved ways to navigate challenging or absurd workplace interactions. This is a way of getting our point across and laughing at the everyday quirks of corporate life without stepping on toes or stirring unnecessary conflict.

Consider this example for the coworker who always thinks they know it all: "I'm sorry, I didn't realize you were an expert on this subject. Please, continue to enlighten us with your wisdom." See what I did there? It's a nice, cheeky way of saying maybe—just maybe—they're not as bright as they think they are, without actually saying it.

Take these witty retorts as office humor initiation secret codes, designed to remark on pesky behaviors without offending or creating unnecessary tension.

Over the years, I've experienced my fair share of unsavory office challenges–from the coworker who always replies 'to all' just to express their gratitude to the world indefinitely, to the one who makes Comic Sans his go-to font for all critical high-priority memos, it's a miracle that anything gets done at work.

And here we are, stumbling through meetings, email miscues, and seemingly infinite spreadsheets with astonishing finesse. Throughout this book, you'll learn infinite examples, advice, and tricks for handling common workplace annoyances with humor, tact, and HR-sanctioned phrases.

Organized in convenient chapters about everything from micromanaging supervisors to email diplomacy mistakes, this book will accompany you through the interactions of your workplace with poise, at the same time preserving your mind. The strength of smart humor and clever communication is immense, and becoming accomplished at it really makes your business life richer.

Reading between the lines is fun, but explicit statements are my preference. If you've got problems, let's discuss them directly to keep communication simple.Here are some examples:

- You're doing a fine job highlighting problems—can we discuss solutions today?
- Your negativity deserves an Oscar—but let's put up some positivity for nomination as well.
- The office thermostat called—it's willing to negotiate. Maybe complaints should come with a complimentary solution attached?

Let's address issues constructively by suggesting improvements and solutions.

Integrity is doing the right thing, even when no one is watching. Ethics is knowing the difference between what you have a right to do and what is right to do. Professional conduct is not simply about following rules; it is about setting a standard of excellence. It is our actions that determine our character, both inside and outside the workplace. Let us strive to create a culture of openness and trust in everything we do.

Just remember the saying, "With great power comes great responsibility." (Voltaire)

Use these lines wisely, maintain professionalism, and always be mindful of the fact that HR is listening.

Welcome to the delightfully absurd, humor-infused, and entirely HR-compliant world of handling workplace absurdities—one witty response at a time.

ONE

COMMUNICATION & INTERPERSONAL CONFLICTS

We've all been there, trapped in a conference room, maybe questioning the meaning of life, while a coworker passionately argues about the font chosen for our presentation slide. Office communication is a thrilling circus of confusion and unclear directions. You also get the occasional email that makes you wonder about the collective IQ of humanity. In any office, communication is a constant back-and-forth where words often lead to misunderstandings.

THE ROLE OF COMMUNICATION IN THE WORKPLACE

Good communication is key for productivity and teamwork, even when it feels like you're trying to get a group of people who aren't quite on the same page to work together. This chapter will give you the tools to navigate tricky workplace situations. You'll learn to read between the lines, understand confusing emails, and use words effectively to respond.

THE POWER OF MINDFUL COMMUNICATION

As the Haas School of Business' Center for Equity, Gender and Leadership suggests, mindful communication is about awareness and intention, ensuring your message lands as intended. It's about connecting, not merely following rules. So get comfortable, grab your coffee, and let's dive into how to say what you mean—or at least, give it your best shot.

SHIFTING FROM PROBLEMS TO SOLUTIONS

Workplace misunderstandings pop up everywhere, like motivational posters in the break room. They often arise from assumptions, unclear directions, and autocorrect mishaps turning simple messages offensive. The key is to focus on solutions instead of problems. Rather than dwelling on what went wrong, think about how to fix it.

IDENTIFYING NEEDS AND FINDING COMMON GROUND

Conflicts often arise because someone doesn't feel heard or valued. Taking time to understand what everyone really wants creates a foundation for finding solutions. It isn't about compromise; it's about establishing common ground where everyone's needs are acknowledged and respected.

THE IMPORTANCE OF ACTIVE LISTENING

Listening is critical. It's not just about hearing the words someone says but understanding their motivations and emotions. It means putting aside your own thoughts to genuinely understand another person's viewpoint. After identifying everyone's needs and listening to their perspectives, try to solve the problem together.

WHEN CONFLICTS ESCALATE

Disagreements can get heated. When that happens, take a break to let emotions cool. Stepping away allows everyone to return with clearer minds. If necessary, involve a neutral third party to mediate the conversation.

LET'S GET REAL SCENARIOS

The Let's Get Real Scenarios throughout the book offer different responses designed to showcase both lighthearted and straightforward approaches; the third bullet always includes a direct option. The direct option allows for clear and unambiguous communication, especially when a light-hearted approach may not be appropriate.

Mysterious Memo:
You get a memo from your boss that's so vague it reads like a riddle. Rather than mutely scratch your head, you respond with a grin, "Appreciate the cryptic approach—it adds a fun escape-room vibe! Mind giving me the decoder key so I can crack this one?" Using a light tone like this will probably get a smile from them and they will likely give you clear directions without feeling awkward.

- "Your memos are becoming my favorite workplace mystery series—any hints for solving today's episode?"
- "This memo reads like corporate poetry—can we do a quick analysis to make sure I'm not missing any metaphors?"
- "Appreciate the creative briefing, but can we quickly translate this into plain English for clarity's sake?"

Email Avalanche:
So, your inbox is suddenly flooded with a bunch of emails from different colleagues and they're all saying different things, leaving you confused and needing to calm things down. You can send a group text with a bit of humor like this: "My inbox feels like a reality show—full

of drama and conflicting storylines. Can we meet briefly to decide the finale?" Using a playful joke like that will likely get everyone laughing and make them more open to questions and working together.

- "My email inbox thinks it's a debate tournament—mind if we quickly pick a winner?"
- "This email thread is starting to feel like a telephone game. Can we regroup and find the original message?"
- "Looks like we have a lot of perspectives—I vote for less inbox ping-pong and a quick video huddle to align."

Unintentional Offense:
Imagine your colleague says something that's unintentionally insensitive during a group meeting, and you can feel the tension in the air. Later on, try talking to them privately, with a smile, and say, "I think that comment might've missed its intended landing spot—mind if we talk it through so we're both on the same page?" By approaching the conversation with empathy, you can keep things light and avoid a strained interaction.

- "That comment might've been on the wrong frequency—can we quickly retune our signals?"
- "I think your joke had some unintended special effects—let's discuss the director's cut version privately."
- "Your comment landed differently than I think you intended. Can we briefly unpack it together?"

Conflicting Priorities:
Two departments are fighting over resources, both of which are asking to be prioritized. In a gesture of diffusion of tension, you call both departments under the tongue-in-cheek sign: "Battle of the Priorities: A Friendly Match to Decide Who Really Wins." The use of friendly colloquial language is an invitation to transparency, excludes irritation, and invites accommodation.

- "Looks like our priorities are playing tug-of-war—can we huddle up and pick the winning team?"
- "Our departments seem stuck in a game of priority ping-pong—let's take a quick timeout to agree on the rules."
- "We've got competing priorities doing their best impressions of emergencies. Shall we sort them calmly together?"

Lost in Translation:
Two departments are fighting over resources, neither of which seem to understand the other's needs. Intent to put out fires, you call both departments under the tongue-in-cheek sign: "Lost in Translation: The Sequel—Now with subtitles and visual aids!" Using informal language can sometimes promote openness, minimize conflict, and encourage cooperation.

- "Our emails are playing an intense telephone game—let's hop on a quick call and get subtitles turned on."
- "Feels like we're communicating across oceans—literally. Let's visualize this together so we speak the same language."
- "We might have accidentally invented a new language between us. Shall we decode it together?"

Ultra Micromanaging:
Your boss is a close watcher of even the smallest tasks. You make the joke in jest during one of their status updates: "Would you prefer daily updates, hourly updates, or should I just livestream my workday?" Your tongue-in-cheek remark implicitly expresses your need for autonomy, and your boss relaxes on the control.

- "Do you want a front-row seat, or would occasional highlight reels of my tasks be okay?"
- "Want to officially join the project, or are you happy coaching from the sidelines?"
- "Appreciate your attention to detail! How about we schedule checkpoints so I can keep you updated without the surprise visits?"

Constant Interruptions:

You're making an important point during a team meeting when your coworker interrupts you again, swerving your thoughts. Rather than seething silently, you crack a warm smile and tease, "I'm glad you're excited—let me just finish formulating my thought before it escapes me again." Your friendly humor nicely reminds them to let you finish.

- "Wow, my sentences must be irresistible today—they keep getting snatched mid-air!"
- "Hold on, my thoughts haven't quite landed yet. Just give me two more seconds to get them safely grounded."
- "I'd appreciate finishing my point first; then, I'm eager to hear your perspective."

Passive-Aggressive Communication:

Your colleague sends you a second ambiguous message, replete with friendly but vague innuendos. Rather than leaving it hanging, you instantly shoot back playfully, "Your messages feel like crossword clues—care to share the answer key?" Your lighthearted joke playfully invites open, tension-free communication.

- "These emails might qualify as abstract art—any chance I could get a simpler version for everyday viewing?"
- "Your emails are like a puzzle. I appreciate the mental workout, but can we simplify just a bit?"
- "To avoid any misinterpretation, could we briefly discuss this directly?"

Rudeness or Condescension:

In a team report, your superior makes a sarcasm-laden comment about your presentation, and there is an uneasy silence. Instead of becoming bristly defensive, you switch to a genial smile and retort quickly, "Glad my presentation added some unexpected excitement! Happy to chat specifics if needed." Your positive, restorative humor resolves the tension without directly addressing their tone.

- "Glad I could provide some comic relief—maybe next time I'll add popcorn!"
- "Happy to keep everyone awake with my unique presenting style!"
- "I'd welcome constructive feedback if there's something specific you'd like me to adjust."

These examples demonstrate how clear communication can turn around those awkward workplace squabbles—you know, the kind where you passive-aggressively contemplate microwaving fish in the office kitchen to make your point. You can address misunderstandings with empathy, curiosity, and a laser focus on solutions. Not just blaming that one person from accounting.

By taking a new approach, you can influence a workplace where diverse viewpoints aren't just tolerated but actually valued, even if those viewpoints include questionable taste in lunch choices. Effective communication isn't about dodging conflict altogether; it's about navigating it with grace and a healthy dose of humor knowing that with the right tools and mindset, any communication breakdown can be a hilariously awkward step towards success. And if all else fails, there's always the option of group therapy, preferably with snacks.

CHAPTER 1 QUIZ: HOW SHOULD YOU HANDLE THESE SCENARIOS?

1. You receive a memo from your manager that is so vague it feels like a puzzle. What's your best approach?

2. Your inbox is flooded with contradictory emails from multiple coworkers. How should you manage this confusion?

3. A coworker unintentionally makes an insensitive remark during a meeting, causing discomfort. What's the appropriate next step?

4. Two departments are arguing fiercely about resource allocation. How can you ease this tension?

5. Language barriers with an international team are causing project confusion. What's a good way to address this?

Answers available at the back of the book.

TWO
PERFORMANCE & RESPONSIBILITY ISSUES

This chapter will resonate with anyone who's ever been stuck on a team with someone who acts like getting things done is just not part of their job description. Weird, right? These are the underperformers, the deadline-missers, and the responsibility-shirkers who make you wonder if they've ever heard of basic teamwork. This chapter is here to arm you with the tools and a hefty dose of humor to navigate these situations with a little bit of fun and a whole lot of finesse.

UNDERSTANDING AND ADDRESSING PERFORMANCE ISSUES

The workplace is like a giant mixed bag of people, skills, and personalities, from creativity and ambition to the occasional setbacks that inevitably arise. Performance is a real thing. It's what keeps the wheels turning. But even in the midst of all this, some people make avoiding work seem like an actual talent. These are the people you'll find loitering by the coffee machine or deep in a conversation about last night's game. They have a gift, it seems, for slipping through the cracks of responsibility.

Few things in the office are more annoying than a coworker who seems to hate deadlines. It's like they're missing the gene for time management. Addressing coworkers who underperform, miss deadlines, avoid accountability, or neglect duties requires a mix of tact, empathy, and a good sense of humor. Without humor, performance management can quickly become a boring cycle of meetings and reviews. The secret is using good communication, setting clear expectations, and maybe using a bit of humor for things that get tense.

IDENTIFYING THE UNDERLYING CAUSE OF POOR PERFORMANCE

If a coworker is underperforming, it's best to be understanding. It's a common problem that can be frustrating and take up time to figure out why they aren't performing well. Is it a motivation problem, a lack of skills, or is something personal happening outside of work? Understanding the reason can help you respond in the right way.

SETTING CLEAR EXPECTATIONS AND CULTIVATING ACCOUNTABILITY

When it comes to performance, clear expectations are key. Make sure you define what you expect in terms of projects, deadlines, and the quality of work. This clarity avoids confusion and ensures everyone is on the same page. Regular check-ins are a good way to track progress and give feedback. There's also a chance to offer support, find any issues, and celebrate progress, no matter how small.

Accountability is essential, but let's be honest—the word "accountability" can make people cringe. Instead of making it feel like a burden, make it feel like a good thing.

LEVERAGING HUMOR TO EASE TENSION

A well-timed joke or lighthearted comment can relieve tension and make difficult conversations easier. But ensure you don't use humor to the point that it undermines the seriousness of an issue. Good humor should never make someone the target of a joke and should always be respectful. When used correctly, humor can help build teams and create a better workplace overall. Next, let's get into some of the scenario-specific tools you can use.

LET'S GET REAL SCENARIOS

Chronic Procrastinator:
You're stuck with someone who views deadlines as soft targets, always having you dashing around at the eleventh hour. Instead of losing your cool, you comment with a smile, "Your deadlines love scenic routes—do you need help drawing a map to the end line?" Your playful way of presenting the issue makes it more likely to address the underlying problem without a fight.

- "Deadlines aren't suggestions—unless we're moving to an artistic interpretation of due dates?"
- "Our project is starting to look like it's practicing yoga—very flexible deadlines. Let's tighten things up!"
- "Let's set clear milestones to ensure we stay on track and avoid last-minute stress."

Dodger:
At team meetings, your colleague skillfully refuses to take ownership, always blaming others when deadlines are missed. Rather than becoming irritated, you bring in a project tracking program employed by everyone with a humorously phrased comment, "This tool helps ensure credit and blame get distributed equally—it's democracy, work-place-style!" Your light-hearted tone playfully enforces responsibility.

- "Let's make accountability our team's newest trend—much better than finger-pointing!"
- "I think our project needs fewer scapegoats and more clear responsibilities—what do you think?"

- "Implementing transparent tracking can help everyone stay aligned and accountable."

Blame Shifter:

You have a coworker who always deflects the blame as soon as something goes wrong. Instead of engaging in a battle of blame, you smile and wisecrack with a chuckle, "We might break the record for fastest finger-pointing—how about we slow down and find solutions instead?" Your humor diplomatically nudges your colleague toward accountability.

- "Our team meetings shouldn't feel like episodes of 'Whodunnit'—let's all play detective less and problem-solver more."
- "Finger-pointing might burn calories, but solutions get us results faster."
- "Let's clarify roles upfront to improve accountability and avoid confusion moving forward."

Invisible Employee:

You notice a colleague habitually vanishes whenever the workload increases. Instead of quietly getting irritated, this time, you mention it in a playful manner: "Your disappearing acts are impressive—but we need your starring role for the whole show." Your lighthearted tone encourages them to understand the importance of their role and return to work.

- "I think we accidentally activated your invisibility cloak during crunch time—let's disable it next deadline."
- "We'd love to see more of you in our meetings—not just your empty chair's excellent attendance record!"
- "Your consistent presence makes a big difference—let's talk about ways to improve engagement during key moments."

Skill Gap:

You observe an employee consistently having trouble with some tasks and impacting team performance. Rather than criticizing, you extend with a grin, "Looks like this task is giving you a tough time—want to tag-team it or call in backup?" Your warm humor encourages the exchange of helpful information and coaching.

- "Don't fight with your spreadsheets alone—let's bring in reinforcements."
- "Even superheroes need sidekicks sometimes. Happy to lend a hand!"
- "If you're feeling stuck, I can help find resources or training to make this task easier."

Perpetual Excuse Maker:
Your coworker is always ready with some reason or another for not finishing work, from slow machines to distracting environments. Instead of calling them out directly, you joke lightheartedly, "Your computer seems to have a personal vendetta against deadlines—how about we troubleshoot together?" Your humor doesn't get derailed by excuses.

- "If your laptop keeps sabotaging us, maybe it's time for an intervention?"
- "Our project's becoming a soap opera—full of drama and endless excuses. Let's rewrite the script!"
- "Let's identify obstacles together and create a practical plan to overcome them."

Overloaded Multitasker:
Your coworker is always willing to take on more work than they can possibly handle, which means their output is sloppy. You approach them with a joke, "Looks like your to-do list might be plotting a rebellion—want help taming it?" This light-hearted offer invites your coworker to prioritize without defensiveness.

- "Your calendar looks busier than Times Square—can I help streamline things?"

- "Maybe it's time we stage a friendly intervention before your task list gains sentience."
- "I'm happy to help prioritize tasks so you can stay focused on what matters most."

Perfectionist's Paralysis:

Your coworker spends too much time perfecting minor details, and you're held up. Playfully, you remark, "Your work belongs in an art gallery—but let's aim for 'great' instead of 'masterpiece' so we can actually deliver on time." Your teasing encourages practicality without compromising their dedication.

- "We love your attention to detail, but perfection might be overspending our deadline's budget."
- "Let's keep things excellent yet achievable—our clients appreciate finished work, not just flawless drafts."
- "I appreciate your high standards, but let's balance detail with meeting deadlines."

Distraction Magnet:

Your coworker has a habit of going off on tangents in conversation, leading discussions down unrelated paths. Smiling cordially, you joke, "I enjoy your scenic conversational detours—let's just save them for after we've crossed today's finish line." This playful refocusing of their attention works.

- "Love the bonus content—but maybe we can hold the behind-the-scenes footage until after our main presentation?"
- "Your ideas are gold—but can we stick to one topic at a time so I don't get conversational whiplash?"
- "Let's stay focused for now and set aside time later to explore additional ideas."

Quality Control Crisis:

Your partner tends to work too quickly, making unnecessary errors.

You lightly tease, "Your drafts have great suspense—I never know which errors I'll find next! Want help making it less thrilling?" The tone of tease encourages repair without embarrassment.

- "Your report has character—mostly typos, but still. Want me to help smooth out some rough edges?"
- "Fast is fun, but accuracy gets applause—how about we slow down just enough to enjoy both?"
- "Quality is critical—let's take a bit more time upfront to reduce revisions later."

Performance Issues: Let's Pretend to Care

When you're dealing with performance issues, the best thing to do is allegedly be proactive. That means showing you care—even if it's just pretending. Clear communication and setting realistic expectations can make a difference, at least on paper. Cultivating a culture of accountability might sound tedious, but it's worth pretending to try.

Using humor can be helpful because, let's be honest, we're all secretly dying inside. Compassion (basically, just forced niceness), a little humor, and understanding—even though we know it's limited—can go a long way when you're addressing these issues. This way, the workplace can at least become respectful, even if everyone is just counting down to the weekend.

CHAPTER 2 QUIZ: HOW SHOULD YOU HANDLE THESE SCENARIOS?

1. Your coworker treats deadlines as flexible suggestions, leaving tasks unfinished until the last minute. How do you humorously yet constructively address their procrastination?

2. A colleague frequently avoids responsibility during meetings and shifts blame elsewhere. What's a humorous way to encourage accountability?

3. A team member consistently disappears when workloads become heavy, causing frustration. How can you lightly address their absence?

4. Your coworker struggles regularly with specific tasks, affecting overall performance. What's a friendly yet helpful way to approach them?

5. A teammate regularly rushes tasks, resulting in frequent errors. How do you gently and humorously suggest focusing more on quality?

Answers available at the back of the book.

THREE
RESPECT & PERSONAL BOUNDARIES

Imagine, you're at your desk wrestling with a spreadsheet that's probably plotting against you when a coworker decides that now is the perfect time to lean over your shoulder and comment on your screensaver. Like seriously, it's a classic case of boundary-crossing, the kind that makes you contemplate a career change to become a professional hermit who only communicates via carrier pigeon.

Respect and boundaries are the silent heroes that keep the peace in any office, or at least prevent complete anarchy. Office life without boundaries can be as irritating as listening to the click-clack of 100,000 tiny hammers banging on a keyboard, or as simple as listening to muffled conversations about weekend plans you're definitely not invited to. Either way, being bombarded by a symphony of invading sounds is real chaos.

SETTING AND MAINTAINING HEALTHY BOUNDARIES

Having healthy boundaries at work helps us stay mentally well and avoid burnout. It's about taking care of ourselves first and balancing work with our personal lives, which can feel like balancing a pot of spaghetti on a unicycle. But if you do it right, it can lead to a more productive and fulfilling work life. Setting boundaries involves knowing what your boundaries are, making sure they don't negatively affect others, and communicating them well. It's like drawing a line in the sand and saying, "This is my space, and I need you to respect it."

HANDLING DISRESPECTFUL BEHAVIOR, HARASSMENT, AND MAINTAINING HEALTHY PROFESSIONAL AND PERSONAL BOUNDARIES

Imagine you're in a meeting and someone makes a joke at your expense. It was supposed to be funny, but it just falls flat. Everyone else laughs uncomfortably, and you feel like you're the punchline of a bad joke. This is when you need to know how to handle disrespectful or hurtful behavior. It's about dealing with the situation professionally while also making it clear that this kind of behavior isn't okay.

When faced with boundary-crossing behavior, the first thing to do is stay calm, even if you really want to say something snarky. By keeping your cool, you allow for a productive conversation instead of a fight. It's about being a diplomat and trying to resolve the situation, not get revenge.

ADDRESSING THE ISSUE DIRECTLY AND PROFESSIONALLY

Once you've calmed down, it's time to talk to the person directly about the issue. Schedule a private conversation where you can openly share your feelings and concerns, and speak from the heart using "I" statements about how their actions affected you. Focus on your experience rather than blaming them. For example, you could say, "I was disappointed when that joke was made in the meeting. It made me feel discouraged and made it harder for me to do my job well." This is a clear way to state your message and start a conversation that leads to understanding.

PRACTICAL STRATEGIES FOR BOUNDARY SETTING

Setting boundaries is like a key piece to the respect puzzle at work. It's really about understanding what your limits are and communicating those limits to your coworkers. Workplace Strategies for Mental Health suggests that you need to set the line, have a plan, and actually respect that boundary you set. It's about building a system that protects your mental and emotional well-being so you can do your best at work. Try using strategies like managing your time well, cutting out distractions, and getting comfortable saying no. These things let you take ownership of your workspace and focus on tasks that actually matter to you. It's about finding that sweet spot so you can succeed in both your work life and personal life without sacrificing one for the other.

LET'S GET REAL SCENARIOS

Overbearing Office Mate:
You're working quietly when your cubicle neighbor leans over your area again, poised to criticize your desktop or email. Instead of losing your temper, you lightly remark, "Should I start charging rent for desk visits, or can we agree on some space boundaries?" Your light-hearted comment politely suggests the issue.

- "Did we merge desks without me knowing?"
- "Are you auditing my workspace, or is this just a friendly inspection?"
- "I appreciate your suggestions, but I'd prefer more personal workspace to stay focused."

Serial Interruptor:
You're about to present your argument in a meeting when a coworker interrupts you again. You graciously smile and say, "Our conversations are turning into duets—can I finish my solo first?" Your quip tactfully encourages more thoughtful listening.

- "If interrupting were a sport, you'd be the champion."

- "Maybe we can save your comments for the director's cut version?"
- "Let's find a system that allows everyone to finish their thoughts clearly."

Office Gossip:
A colleague starts sharing office rumors again. You smile politely and respond, "Thanks, but I canceled my subscription to workplace gossip."

- "Sounds interesting, but my gossip meter is already maxed out."
- "My drama quota is full—got anything productivity-related?"
- "I'd prefer if we kept conversations positive and work-focused."

Inappropriate Jokester:
Your colleague makes another awkward joke in a meeting. You briefly respond, "Careful, HR might ask you to guest-star in their next training video."

- "Is this a comedy special, or should we tone it down?"
- "Your jokes always spice things up—maybe keep the spice workplace-appropriate?"
- "Let's aim for humor that's comfortable for everyone."

Boundary Pusher:
Your boss often emails you late-night requests. The next morning, you reply, "Looks like your message arrived after my work-life boundaries kicked in, but I'll have this for you today."

- "My notifications go offline after hours—sorry for the delay!"
- "Night-time emails require premium subscription—I'm only basic tier."

- "In the interest of balance, let's keep work discussions during regular hours."

Boundary-Crossing Screen Watcher:
A coworker frequently glances at your monitor while you're working. You turn with a playful smile and say, "Should I start charging admission fees, or can we agree to keep eyes on our own screens?"

- "Want a tour of my screen, or just window-shopping?"
- "Curious about my desktop decor, or genuinely needing something?"
- "If you need something, just let me know directly—I'd appreciate more privacy."

After-Hours Texter:
Your coworker regularly texts after work hours. The next morning you respond warmly, "My notifications clocked out early yesterday—catching up now!"

- "After-hours texts are against my phone's union rules."
- "Looks like your message arrived after my brain powered down."
- "To keep a healthy work-life balance, let's stick to communication during working hours."

Okay, so here's the deal: it's all about balance. Like a tightrope walker, you know you have to be clear and direct when someone's being disrespectful, while also showing you understand where they're coming from. By responding to disrespect and having good boundaries, you create a workplace where everyone feels valued and their space is respected. We want a place where everyone feels heard and can do their best work every day. So, even if you feel you have annoying coworkers, building a great workplace starts with you and the boundaries you put in place. We all know the often used cliche, it's not a sprint, but a marathon, so you have to keep at it—like someone maintaining the office vibe.

CHAPTER 3 QUIZ: HOW SHOULD YOU HANDLE THESE SCENARIOS?

1. Your coworker frequently leans over your workspace to critique your desktop or emails. What's a humorous way to gently communicate your need for personal space?

2. A colleague repeatedly interrupts you during meetings. How can you humorously encourage them to allow you to finish speaking?

3. Your coworker begins sharing workplace rumors again. What's a friendly yet clear way to discourage office gossip?

4. A team member consistently makes inappropriate jokes during meetings. What's a playful but firm way to encourage appropriate humor?

5. Your supervisor often sends late-night work messages. How can you humorously reinforce healthy work-life boundaries?

Answers available at the back of the book.

FOUR

TOXIC BEHAVIOR & NEGATIVE ATTITUDES

R eally bad office cultures translate to places that have you second-guessing your career choices every single Monday. It can look like being exhausted by the thought of dealing with that super cynical person in the next cubicle who finds something wrong with everything, or the office gossip who always spreads rumors like wildfire. It's like these folks were just born under a dark cloud and want to bring everyone else down with them.

UNDERSTANDING THE IMPACT OF TOXIC BEHAVIOR

Dealing with negativity at work can feel like trying to solve a really frustrating puzzle where none of the pieces seem to fit. It's about figuring out what's actually causing the negativity, understanding the things that make a workplace toxic, and then creating practices that encourage respect and teamwork.

RECOGNIZING FORMS OF WORKPLACE NEGATIVITY

Workplace negativity and toxicity can show up in so many ways, from those subtle passive-aggressive comments to straight-up bullying and harassment—you know, those coworkers who are always criticizing every project, who seem to enjoy finding fault, and who appear to get a kick out of bringing others down. Let's take a look at some ways you can handle some of the most difficult situations with grace and keep your sanity intact while at work.

Imagine heading to work on a beautiful sunny morning, only to get there and find that a coworker's mood is as dark as a storm cloud about to burst. Their negativity hangs over the place like a thick fog, bringing down the whole office. You have to figure out how to work with these types of people without letting their negativity spread and poison the entire workplace.

ESTABLISHING CLEAR AND CONSISTENT BOUNDARIES

One of the best ways to deal with toxic coworkers is to set clear boundaries and stick to them consistently and firmly. Indeed's guide on handling toxic coworkers says that setting boundaries and distancing yourself from negativity are essential for protecting your physical and emotional well-being. Often, negativity happens when someone isn't feeling interested or satisfied with their job.

According to the Indeed editorial team, it's crucial to recognize when negativity starts affecting your mood and to clearly communicate your limits. This could be as simple as not spending too much time on that negative person, changing the subject when they get stuck on something, or just ending conversations early before they drain your energy.

COMBATING WORKPLACE GOSSIP AND BULLYING

Workplace gossip can be really toxic, right? It can totally wreck team morale and trust in a heartbeat. It often happens when people don't feel like they're in the loop or know what's going on. To stop gossip from spreading, the Society for Human Resource Management suggests that everyone should be taught how harmful gossip is and have some clear rules.

Bullying at work is seriously harmful, and probably the worst kind of toxic behavior. It can be incredibly damaging to the people targeted and to the whole company. Bullying can look like intimidation, harassment, or just plain verbal aggression, and can lead to low morale, stress, and even legal issues.

FOSTERING LONG-TERM CHANGE

When you're dealing with toxic behavior, it's important to remember that things don't change overnight. It takes effort from everyone. But by figuring out the root causes, setting clear boundaries, and creating a culture of respect and openness, it's totally possible to build a workplace where positivity thrives and employees can do their best work.

LET'S GET REAL SCENARIOS

Eternal Pessimist:
Your coworker constantly complains about every new project, which brings down the morale of the team. Instead of quietly taking it, you joke, "If pessimism were an Olympic sport, you'd be undefeated—but how about helping us score some positivity points?" Your humorous approach helps him rethink his approach without you getting into a confrontation.

- "Your inner critic deserves a vacation—let's book it a trip."
- "You're great at finding clouds—let's start looking for silver linings."
- "Constructive feedback is valuable—let's focus on solutions to improve outcomes."

Gossip Guru:
Another colleague constantly translates office rumors into soap opera storylines, creating unnecessary tension. Instead of playing along, you diplomatically deflect, chuckling warmly while you add, "our office drama could win Daytime Emmys—but how about we save spoilers

and stick to facts?" Humor helps you deflect to a culture of openness over gossip.

- "Your stories rival daytime TV—but maybe let's save drama for after-hours."
- "You're our in-house gossip columnist—maybe focus more on good news?"
- "Let's keep conversations focused on factual information to avoid misunderstandings."

Overbearing Bully:

A senior colleague continues to intimidate other employees through bullying or scornful behavior. Instead of going along quietly, you remain firm but calm and say, "I didn't realize intimidation was on today's meeting agenda—let's try collaboration instead." Your assertive humor sets reasonable boundaries without warming up the situation.

- "Your management style feels like boot camp—can we aim for team-building exercises instead?"
- "We prefer pep talks over put-downs—care to join us?"
- "Respectful communication is key. Let's ensure everyone feels heard and valued."

Passive-Aggressive Pro:

Your colleague persistently tosses veiled put-downs disguised as compliments, leaving you confused and uneasy. You counter with firmness by saying, "I admire your skill in compliments—they always keep us guessing. Mind aiming for clarity next time?" Your gentle touch defuses tension and promotes greater clarity of communication.

- "Your backhanded compliments are practically an art form, but directness might work better."
- "Reading between the lines is fun, but clear statements are my favorite."
- "If you have concerns, let's discuss them directly to keep communication clear."

Energy Vampire:
You have a colleague who is known for always being a drain on meeting energy with endless complaints and negativity. Instead of tolerating it without saying anything, you humorously suggest, "Your gloomy predictions deserve their own Netflix special—but maybe we start meetings with good news first?" This lighthearted response refocuses attention on positivity.

- "You're great at highlighting problems—can we focus on solutions today?"
- "Your negativity is Oscar-worthy, but let's nominate some positivity too."
- "To keep meetings productive, let's lead with positive updates and actionable solutions."

Chronic Complainer:
Your coworker always finds something wrong, from the office snacks to the room temperature. Instead of quietly dealing with their negativity, you give a playful response, "Your complaint skills are unmatched. Ready to switch sides and champion solutions?" Your humor makes them aware that they need more constructive contributions.

- "The office thermostat called—it's willing to negotiate."
- "Maybe complaints should come with a complimentary solution attached?"
- "Let's address issues constructively by suggesting improvements and solutions."

Look, the key to a less annoying workplace isn't rocket science. It's about figuring out what's causing all the grumbling and making sure everyone treats each other decently. If you set some ground rules, actually talk to each other like adults, and celebrate the wins, you can create a work environment that's more fun than a barrel of monkeys—and without all the mess. Just remember that tackling negativity isn't a solo mission. It takes a team effort and a genuine desire to build a work environment where everyone feels like they belong.

CHAPTER 4 QUIZ: HOW SHOULD YOU HANDLE THESE SCENARIOS?

1. Your coworker constantly highlights flaws in every initiative, dampening team enthusiasm. How can you gently address their persistent negativity with humor?

2. A colleague regularly spreads office gossip, causing unnecessary tension. How do you humorously redirect the conversation toward factual information?

3. A senior coworker often uses aggressive tactics that intimidate others. What's an assertive yet humorous way to encourage respectful collaboration?

4. Your coworker consistently delivers subtle insults disguised as compliments. How can you humorously request clearer, more direct communication?

5. A team member habitually complains about everything from snacks to room temperature. How can you humorously encourage them to provide constructive solutions instead?

Answers available at the back of the book.

FIVE
ETHICS & PROFESSIONAL CONDUCT

ntegrity isn't just some buzzword to throw around in a meeting. It's the foundation of a productive and respectful workplace. Every choice we make, no matter how small, has an impact on the organization, like the effects of a motivational speech that's gone totally sideways. Think of this chapter as your guide to navigating the sometimes tricky world of ethics with a smile, a bit of sarcasm, and a whole lot of common sense.

MANAGING UNETHICAL CONDUCT, DISHONESTY, AND INTEGRITY IN THE WORKPLACE

Okay, let's be honest: dishonesty at work feels like a sneaky ninja creeping in and causing trouble before you even know it. You get caught off guard every time. It's that coworker who forgets to tell you about their part in a project that flopped, or the team leader who steals your brilliant idea and takes all the credit. Deception can come in a million different forms, from little white lies to full-blown whoppers that could be the plot of a novel. The tricky part is figuring out how to handle these issues without turning the office into a reality TV show.

CONFRONTING DISHONESTY IN THE WORKPLACE WITH TACT AND EVIDENCE

When you're dealing with dishonesty, it's all about finding the right balance between being tactful and being firm. You need to address the situation directly without making accusations that are going to cause a major blow-up. Start by speaking with the person directly. Use "I" statements to explain how their behavior affected you and potentially the team. Focus on finding a solution instead of just pointing fingers.

HANDLING UNETHICAL PRACTICES PROACTIVELY

Unethical actions, whether they seem small or are really serious, can ruin trust and damage a company's reputation. Integrity issues often pop up when coworkers don't feel connected to the company's values or when they see a disconnect between their personal ethics and where they work. Think about the sales team that stretches the truth to make a deal, or the accounting team that messes with the numbers to meet goals.

Even when things get tough and it's tempting to cut corners, remember that integrity is everything. If you see unethical behavior, try to focus on finding a solution to make things better. Here are some ways to help you communicate.

LET'S GET REAL SCENARIOS

Credit Hog:
In a team meeting, a coworker confidently presents your hard work as their own. You are steaming mad. Rather than confronting them publicly, you gather clear evidence of contributions and discuss it with them privately by lightly remarking, "I loved your presentation—probably because it sounded exactly like the notes I wrote last week. Maybe we can collaborate openly next time?" Your humorous and friendly tone clearly sets expectations without tension.

- "Impressive recall of my ideas—how about giving a co-author credit next time?"
- "Great minds think alike, but let's clarify who thought first."
- "To keep teamwork transparent, I'd appreciate acknowledgement for my contributions."

Creative Borrower:
Your coworker regularly takes credit for the team's ideas and publicly presents them as their own. After another occurrence, you gently joke, "It seems we're sharing a creative wavelength again—maybe next time, we should announce our ideas together?" Your playful tone addresses the issue without confrontation.

- "Are you borrowing everyone's notes, or are we just creatively synced?"
- "We might need to patent our joint ideas—want to co-present next time?"
- "To maintain clarity and fairness, let's openly recognize everyone's input."

Boss's Pet:
Your manager clearly favors one employee, and it's noticeable because they consistently give that employee prime projects and promotions. This is affecting team morale. Rather than silently fuming, you address the situation directly by humorously noting, "It looks like promotions require a secret handshake—mind teaching it to the rest of us?" Your humor sends the message about the importance of transparency.

- "Does the employee of the month title come with a membership card, or can anyone apply?"
- "Your star performer might appreciate some company in the spotlight."
- "Clear criteria for opportunities would help keep morale high and team dynamics balanced."

Corner-Cutter:

A colleague regularly sacrifices quality to meet tight deadlines, and it's jeopardizing the team's reputation. Instead of silently getting upset about it, you approach them gently, joking, "I appreciate speed, but let's avoid the 'fix-it-later' method—it's getting a bit too thrilling." Your friendly humor gently reinforces accountability.

- "Fast work is great, but accuracy deserves some love, too."
- "I admire your efficiency, but let's not give quality the day off."
- "Balancing speed and quality ensures we maintain our team's strong reputation."

Numbers Game:
You discover colleagues in the finance department manipulating numbers to hit targets. You decide to privately raise your ethical concerns with management, humorously remarking, "Looks like our numbers took up creative writing—let's get back to nonfiction." Your gentle tone underscores the seriousness without escalating tension.

- "Financial fiction might be interesting reading, but let's stick to facts."
- "The books don't need a plot twist—accuracy is dramatic enough."
- "Integrity in our reporting is crucial for our credibility and success."

Gossip Whisperer:
A colleague regularly shares confidential information about clients, so you address the issue by saying, "Your leaks are giving office gossip columns a run for their money—let's tighten things up." Your light-hearted approach highlights the importance of confidentiality.

- "Did your confidentiality clause go on vacation?"
- "Your gossip scoop is too hot—maybe stick to cooler, less sensitive topics."

- "Maintaining confidentiality protects trust and ensures professionalism."

Expense-Report Magician:
Your coworker frequently inflates their expense reports. Rather than ignoring the clear ethical issue, you approach them, jokingly saying, "Your receipts are pretty magical lately—should we review the accounting rules before finance does its own magic trick?" This playful yet clear message addresses the issue comfortably.

- "Your expenses might win a creativity award—but accounting prefers facts."
- "Looks like you're pioneering expense reporting innovations —maybe check policy first?"
- "Accuracy in reporting expenses helps maintain our team's integrity."

Meeting Ghost:
A team member consistently skips important meetings without explanation. Rather than openly calling them out, you remark privately afterward, "Missed you again today—should we start booking a hologram, or do you prefer traditional invites?" Your friendly humor gently encourages accountability.

- "Your attendance is becoming legendary—how about joining us in person next time?"
- "Should we send out a search party, or just set extra reminders?"
- "Your participation is valuable. Please prioritize attending future meetings."

Navigating tricky situations at work can be a real minefield, but hey, honesty is usually your best bet. It's like a compass for the office jungle, you know? All these tiny choices you make get you a bit closer to your destination—they might seem small, but they're actually shaping the whole vibe of the workplace. When tensions are high you have to decide: are we going for a team of superheroes or *Lord of the Flies* here? Your actions are like little building blocks to make sure everyone feels valued and ready to conquer the next best thing, or at least their Monday morning emails.

CHAPTER 5 QUIZ: HOW SHOULD YOU HANDLE THESE SCENARIOS?

1. A coworker presents your hard work as their own during a team meeting. How can you address this privately with a bit of humor?

2. Your coworker regularly takes your privately shared ideas and publicly claims credit. What's a humorous yet clear way to address this issue?

3. Your manager clearly favors one employee, affecting team morale. How can you humorously encourage transparency around opportunities?

4. A colleague frequently sacrifices quality to meet deadlines, putting the team's reputation at risk. How can you gently address this concern with humor?

5. You discover colleagues manipulating financial numbers to hit targets. What's a humorous yet serious approach to address this ethically?

Answers available at the back of the book.

A QUICK PAUSE:

Let me take a moment to express that I'm very grateful that you chose to read to this book. Would you mind taking a quick moment to leave a quick review now to pay it forward and help others like you? It will take less than 2-3 minutes.

Not only does this help me improve future resources for you, but it also fuels others on their journey to find HR-approved ways to handle challenging workplace conversations without landing themselves in trouble.

Would you be so kind as to scan the QR code to share your thoughts?

Also, visit HRapprovedways.com to access the review page and bonus content.

SIX

BOSS INTERACTIONS & MICROMANAGEMENT

S o, the workplace is like a game show where the big prize is getting a paycheck and keeping your sanity. Think of your boss as the host. They've got all the cards, and you're just trying to make it through the day. Some bosses are great, like good back support, but some are as frustrating as a missing puzzle piece. This chapter is your guide to dealing with boss relationships, especially those dreaded micromanagers.

FACING THE MICROMANAGER MICROSCOPE

Micromanaging, as Rebecca Knight has painted the picture in her write-up on working for such bosses, feels like surgery from an extremely shaky surgeon's hand. It's constant watching, hovering, and just plain intrusion. You start feeling more like a science experiment than a professional. If you're nodding your head along because you felt that suffocating feeling from a micromanager, you know exactly how annoying it is to always be second-guessed. But don't worry, understanding why micromanagers act like that is the first step to making things better.

Usually, micromanagement comes from a place of insecurity or a need to control everything. It's a manager's attempt to get things perfect, but at the cost of your independence and usually your morale. The result is a toxic work environment where people feel like they're being held back instead of valued. The best way to get out of that kind of situation is to build communication and trust with your boss. You need to help them zoom out from the microscope and see the big picture. We'll talk about some specific ways of dealing with this.

TECHNIQUES FOR EFFECTIVELY HANDLING DIFFICULT SUPERVISORS, MICROMANAGERS

Working with a difficult boss can feel like trying to tame a wild animal with some duct tape and a prayer. It's really about finding the right tools that will make the biggest impact. You know, you have to stand up for yourself but also keep things respectful.

One of the best things you can do is set some clear boundaries. Think of it like putting up an invisible fence; it shows where the line is for what's okay and not okay. You could start by talking with your manager and having a real conversation about your role and their expectations. Remember to also discuss the limitations of your role.

Communication is super important when dealing with a micro-manager. Keeping them in the loop with regular progress reports helps ease their worries and gives you some freedom. Try having short regular meetings to talk about projects, what's working, and what problems you fixed. This shows your boss you've got things handled and reduces their urge to control every little thing. Remember, a boss who feels in the know is less likely to micromanage.

Is it possible that you could try to be more understanding with a micromanager? Maybe try to see their point of view. Maybe they're dealing with pressure from their boss or other personal problems. Okay, experience tells me that is probably their issue, not yours, but it doesn't hurt if you try to understand their situation.

MICROMANAGEMENT CAN BE DEMORALIZING AND YOU NEED A PLAN TO HANDLE IT

Micromanagement can feel like you're in a race where the finish line keeps moving, no matter how hard you try. Make sure you have a running record of your work and can communicate that when you've gone above and beyond. This record not only proves what you're capable of, but also lets you communicate your value and how being micromanaged is actually affecting your performance.

IN SEARCH OF SOLUTIONS TO COPE WITH A MICROMANAGER

When looking for ways to deal with a micromanager, try to focus on solutions that are good for both you and the company. For example, you could ask for professional development opportunities or suggest that your assignments be shifted to better use your skills. By talking about growth and development, you can ease your manager's concerns about your performance. Here are some responses that you can use when you're directly faced with micromanagement.

LET'S GET REAL SCENARIOS

Hovering Hawk:
Your boss often hovers nearby, closely monitoring your every move as if expecting you to pull off a magic trick. Rather than getting annoyed, you gently joke, "Thinking of pulling up a chair, or can we set regular check-ins instead?" Your humor reassures your boss and lets them know that you are aware of their lingering presence, while politely advocating for autonomy.

- "Is today's viewing a special feature, or can I continue the regular programming?"
- "Would you prefer a live feed, or should I send highlights later?"

- "I appreciate your attention—let's set up regular updates to streamline the process."

Credit Collector:
Your boss frequently stands next to your desk throughout the day and then claims credit for your ideas during meetings. Instead of quietly fuming, you calmly approach them privately, smiling as you say, "Loved your summary of my work—next time, for my growth and development, I would love to be involved to co-present and make it official?" Your humor highlights your contribution without confrontation.

- "Impressive summary—next time, can we include the author's credits?"
- "Your retelling of my ideas has great flair—how about we present jointly next time?"
- "I appreciate your enthusiasm for my ideas. Next time, I welcome the opportunity to collaborate on the presentation together."

Puppet Master:
Your supervisor insists on controlling every detail of your work, making you feel like a puppet on strings. Rather than showing your frustration, you suggest playfully, "Maybe it's time we cut the puppet strings—think I could audition for a solo act on the next project?" Your friendly tone helps encourage autonomy without causing tension.

- "Should I rehearse my puppet act, or could I take a solo performance this round?"
- "I promise I'll perform even better if you loosen the strings just a little."
- "Let's try giving me more autonomy. I'm confident it will improve my performance."

Unseen Achiever:

Despite your boss's micromanagement, they rarely notice your efforts. Rather than staying frustrated, you proactively schedule a review, humorously saying, "I think my accomplishments turned invisible again—mind if we spotlight them briefly?" Your good-natured approach draws attention positively and constructively.

- "Maybe my work achievements have turned invisible—can we check your visibility settings?"
- "Did my accomplishments slip into stealth mode? Let me share them again clearly."
- "I'd appreciate discussing my recent achievements to ensure alignment and recognition."

Perpetual Critic:
Your manager consistently points out flaws in your work without offering any helpful suggestions. Instead of feeling discouraged, you approach the situation gently, joking, "I see my work inspired another round of commentary—any chance I could get a few spoiler alerts next time?" Your humor gently invites constructive feedback.

- "Your feedback keeps my ego humble—but solutions might boost my confidence even more."
- "You're a master of critique—care to also share the secret recipe for improvement?"
- "Constructive feedback is always welcome—let's identify specific ways I can improve."

Favoritism Fiasco:
Your supervisor clearly favors another employee, awarding them prime opportunities and recognition. Rather than quietly feeling undervalued, you approach your boss calmly and joke, "I must've missed the auditions for favorite employee—mind sharing the application details?" Your humor gently addresses fairness without confrontation.

- "Do I need a VIP membership for the good assignments, or is there a waiting list?"
- "If there's a secret handshake for preferred status, count me in next time!"
- "To ensure fairness, can we set clearer guidelines for assigning opportunities?"

Deadline Dramatist:
Your manager regularly creates urgent tasks right before you're about to leave for the day. Instead of quietly resenting this habit, you jokingly mention, "Our deadlines always have dramatic entrances—can we schedule them earlier to avoid the cliffhangers?" Your humor gently conveys your request for better planning.

- "Deadlines don't need surprise parties—regular invites are just fine."
- "These last-minute requests feel like cliffhangers—can we try a less suspenseful approach?"
- "Consistent scheduling helps everyone stay productive— let's plan deadlines earlier."

Off-the-Clock Messenger:
Your colleague, and someone you consider a friend, was just promoted. You both frequently exchanged texts after work, but now they have started texting you after work about work-related topics. This has blurred the line between office hours and personal time. Instead of feeling pressured to respond immediately, you set a friendly yet firm boundary the next morning:

- "Hey, your text got caught between friend-mode and work-mode. Catching up now!"
- "Looks like your message landed after my brain shifted from colleague to friend."
- "Love chatting with you, but let's save work stuff for when we're both on the clock!"

Goalpost Mover:

Your manager repeatedly changes project objectives mid-stream, causing frustration and confusion. Rather than quietly accepting it, you humorously address the issue by saying, "Our project goals seem to have commitment issues—maybe we can help them settle down this time?" Your friendly approach invites clarity without conflict.

- "These moving targets are giving me whiplash—let's anchor them down."
- "Are our project goals testing their freedom, or can we lock them down soon?"
- "For smoother execution, let's agree on firm project objectives from the start."

Okay, so here's the deal. It's all about walking that tightrope, right? You gotta speak up for yourself, but also, like, try to see things from their perspective—even if they're being completely bonkers. Setting clear boundaries is key. Think of it like putting up a "Do Not Enter" sign, but, you know, in a nice way. Stay open to talking, even if you want to scream. And remember, you've totally got the power to navigate all the weirdness with your boss like a pro. Seriously, you're the captain of your own ship here. So, go make the workplace awesome for you and your crew.

CHAPTER 6 QUIZ: HOW SHOULD YOU HANDLE THESE SCENARIOS?

1. Your boss frequently hovers over your workspace, closely watching your every move. How can you humorously advocate for more autonomy?

2. During meetings, your boss often takes credit for your ideas. How can you politely and playfully address this issue?

3. Your supervisor insists on controlling every detail, making you feel micromanaged. What humorous approach could you use to suggest more independence?

4. Your manager consistently points out flaws without providing helpful suggestions. How can you gently encourage more constructive feedback?

5. Your manager frequently changes project goals mid-stream, causing confusion. How can you address this issue humorously and effectively?

Answers available at the back of the book.

SEVEN
CAREER GROWTH & RECOGNITION

Getting a promotion and moving up the ladder at work can feel like trying to climb a corporate ladder made of wet noodles. For many of us, it's like you're being mocked by those motivational posters with kittens hanging from branches telling you to hang in there. Career growth is what connects your ambition with actually getting things done. But don't worry, this chapter is here to help. Think of it as your guide filled with some humor, a little bit of insight, and a healthy dose of what's actually realistic when it's your time for a promotion.

CONFRONTING ISSUES AROUND DENIED PROMOTIONS, UNCLEAR JOB EXPECTATIONS, AND INADEQUATE ACKNOWLEDGMENT OF CONTRIBUTIONS

You've been working hard, always doing great work, and then you hear the crushing words, "Not this time," when promotions come around. Being denied a promotion can feel really personal, like a slap in the face that tells you your value isn't seen, but this doesn't have to be the end of the story. There are ways to turn this around with clear proactive steps.

SEEKING CLARITY AND CONSTRUCTIVE CRITICISM

We'll get into some specific suggestions on what to say, but start by asking for some clarity and constructive feedback. Set up a private meeting with your manager to really understand what went into their decision. Use this time to ask questions, get clear on expectations, figure out any gaps, and ask for advice on how to improve going forward. This shows that you're committed to growing professionally and helps make sure your goals are in line with what the company wants.

CLARIFYING UNCLEAR JOB EXPECTATIONS

Responsibilities are vague. It's like trying to run a race without knowing the course in advance. Even the most motivated people will struggle. If your job isn't clearly defined, you're not really set up to succeed, and confusion is pretty much guaranteed. So, it's important to politely but firmly ask for each part of your responsibilities, duties, and goals to be clearly defined and measured. Having this kind of clarity helps you connect your actions with real tangible results.

ENHANCING VISIBILITY TO GAIN RECOGNITION

It's a real bummer when you're working hard but no one seems to notice. It can kill your motivation and make you start doubting yourself. To make sure your work gets seen, you've got to be your own advocate, but in a smart way. Keep track of your wins and make sure to highlight the results that have helped the company without being annoying. Share your achievements regularly in team meetings and during performance reviews, so that your contributions are clear and can't be missed. Oh, and did I mention, don't be annoying? Nobody likes THAT coworker.

ENHANCING YOUR PROFESSIONAL PRESENCE

Want to get ahead in your career? It's all about being seen. Try taking on those big noticeable projects and volunteering for the tough jobs. Focusing on getting things done, being proactive, and being a team player really helps you become noticed and respected. Now, it's important to speak up for yourself because everyone should have the recognition they deserve. But what should you do if your company or boss isn't living up to that?

LET'S GET REAL SCENARIOS

Promotion Puzzle:
When the promotion list comes out and your name isn't on it, you're understandably puzzled. Instead of quietly wondering what happened, you approach your manager and humorously remark, "Looks like my promotion got lost in the mail—can we track it down together?" Your friendly approach opens the door for constructive feedback.

- "Did my promotion take a scenic route, or should we talk about directions?"
- "Feels like I'm stuck in promotion traffic—any tips to clear the road?"
- "I'd appreciate discussing specific steps I can take to improve and advance."

Role Riddle:
You've been assigned a task that's outside your typical responsibilities, leaving you feeling confused. Rather than struggling in the dark, you approach your manager and say, "My job description feels like a mystery novel lately—can we clarify the plot?" Your humorous tone encourages open dialogue about role expectations.

- "My role description turned into a choose-your-own-adventure—mind helping pick the right chapter?"

- "It seems my responsibilities became a bit adventurous—let's map them clearly."
- "I'd appreciate some clarity on my responsibilities to ensure I'm aligned with team goals."

Invisible Innovator:
Despite consistently providing unique solutions, your efforts rarely get recognized by leadership. Instead of remaining quietly frustrated, you approach your manager cheerfully: "I think my contributions turned invisible again—mind helping me make them apparent?" Your playful yet clear communication prompts valuable acknowledgment.

- "My latest ideas went stealth mode again—can we turn off invisibility settings?"
- "Did my accomplishments activate ghost mode? Time for a quick spotlight?"
- "I'd appreciate your advice on increasing visibility for my contributions."

Networking Novice:
You realize that your limited connections within your organization might be holding back your growth. Instead of feeling isolated, you jokingly remark to colleagues, "Turns out my network is smaller than my Wi-Fi range—care to help me expand coverage?" Your humor facilitates new conversations, helping you build essential relationships.

- "I think my network is buffering—mind helping me refresh my connections?"
- "My professional circle feels like dial-up internet—let's speed things up!"
- "I'd value your guidance on expanding my internal network to grow professionally."

Feedback Seeker:
You consistently perform well, but meaningful feedback remains elusive. Rather than waiting, you make a joke with your manager,

"Feedback seems scarce lately—should I send out a search party or schedule a meeting?" Your humor gently encourages proactive, constructive conversations.

- "Did my feedback go into spam, or are we just overdue for a chat?"
- "My growth would appreciate regular check-ins, or do we need a treasure map?"
- "I'd like to schedule regular feedback sessions to support my ongoing development."

Job Description Mystery:
You were hired for a specific role, yet your daily tasks constantly shift without clear instructions, leaving you confused and overwhelmed. Rather than quietly stressing, you humorously approach your manager, saying, "My job description is starting to feel like a choose-your-own-adventure story—mind helping me pick the right page?" Your playful tone sets the stage for a clarifying conversation.

- "Feels like my role took a detour—can we get it back on the main road?"
- "My tasks are getting creative—maybe too creative. Could we refocus?"
- "I'd appreciate clarifying my job duties to ensure we're aligned on expectations."

Recognition Black Hole:
You consistently exceed expectations, yet your achievements remain unnoticed by your supervisor. Instead of staying quietly frustrated, you make a joke during a check-in, "I think my accomplishments fell into the office black hole again—any chance we could pull them back into orbit?" Your friendly humor brings attention to your contributions without confrontation.

- "Did my recent wins turn invisible again? Let's try spotlighting them."

- "My achievements might need GPS—they keep missing your radar."
- "I'd appreciate feedback and recognition to help guide my ongoing efforts."

Ladder with Missing Rungs:
You've applied a few times for internal positions, but you keep getting denied or are hitting unclear roadblocks. Rather than becoming discouraged, you meet with your manager and humorously remark, "Feels like my career ladder is missing a few rungs—mind helping me rebuild it?" Your playful approach invites a transparent discussion about advancement.

- "Is my career path under construction? Let's build a clear route."
- "My advancement feels like climbing stairs in the dark—care to shine a light?"
- "Could we discuss actionable steps I can take to advance my career here?"

All right, let's be real here. What's gonna help you actually win at this work thing? It's about speaking up for yourself, even if it feels like you're auditioning for a reality show where your boss is the harshest judge on TV. Ask those questions even if you think they're dumb, because, spoiler alert: they're probably not. These things are like the secret ingredients to making work not suck. You're basically setting yourself up to win the lottery, except the prize is a good work experience, because let's be honest—that's what we all want, right?

CHAPTER 7 QUIZ: HOW SHOULD YOU HANDLE THESE SCENARIOS?

1. You discover your name is missing from the promotion list despite strong performances. How can you address this positively with your manager?

2. Your assigned tasks keep changing unexpectedly, leaving you confused about your responsibilities. What's a humorous way to clarify your role?

3. Your innovative contributions consistently go unnoticed by leadership. How do you gently bring attention to your efforts?

4. You realize your limited internal network might be affecting your career growth. How can you humorously approach colleagues to expand your connections?

5. You've repeatedly exceeded expectations, yet recognition remains elusive. How can you playfully initiate a conversation about receiving acknowledgment?

Answers available at the back of the book.

EIGHT
EMAIL & DIGITAL COMMUNICATION

I f you work at a company, whether you're remote or in the office, it's like instant messages and emails are flying around all day, like confetti at a party. Sometimes, the way we talk online can actually mess up our relationships with our coworkers, even when we don't mean to. Think about it, you're trying to write an email to move a project forward. You're trying to balance your tone, what you need to say, and how you say it. You're hoping your message doesn't come off as passive-aggressive or just plain confusing. It can feel like a high-wire act, and one wrong move can lead to major miscommunication. Before you know it, someone thinks you've sent a nasty email.

EFFECTIVE USE OF CHATS AND DIGITAL MESSAGING PLATFORMS

Since emails aren't going anywhere anytime soon, it's super important to figure out how to avoid mix-ups when sending or receiving them. Because you can't hear someone's tone or see their body language, the person reading your email is going to interpret it using their own feelings, and that can create problems. According to Pollack Peacebuilding Systems, writing emails clearly and keeping them short and structured is key to avoiding misunderstandings. It's all about how you word your message.

Now, the digital messaging and chat apps at work—they're great because you can talk to people quickly like you're face to face, but it's so easy to just click a button. You can quickly connect with team members, share ideas, and even vent about office drama. But these platforms also can cause miscommunication to spiral out of control. A comment that seems harmless can lead to a big misunderstanding faster than you can type "LOL." Remember, emojis and GIFs can help, but don't overdo it, and make sure they make sense or you'll just confuse people.

NAVIGATING CONFLICTS, ETIQUETTE ISSUES, AND MISUNDERSTANDINGS

You're super busy with a project, and your inbox is flooded with messages that need your attention right away. Then, an email pops up from a coworker and the subject line is written in all caps, which makes it seem super urgent. Your heart races, you open it, and it's just a simple request for feedback on a presentation slide. Because the email was in all caps, it has turned a normal message into a computer version of a shouting match.

That's how digital communication works—when you don't have a tone of voice, it can easily lead to unintentional fights and communication blunders. So, how do you get through these electronic minefields? You need to be really aware of communication courtesy and learn how to read between the lines. The key is to approach every conversation with the intention of being clear and understanding. When you write emails, make sure your message has a beginning, a middle, and an end. Make sure your purpose is clear and your tone is polite. Avoid using all caps or too many exclamation points because that can easily make you seem aggressive or overly emotional.

ADDRESSING AND RESOLVING DIGITAL CONFLICTS

When conflicts do happen, it's important to address them face-to-face and professionally. Pollack Peacebuilding Systems suggests that when dealing with a conflict over email, the best approach is to acknowledge the issue, understand everyone's feelings, and then talk about it directly, either over a call or via video conference if needed. This can help release stress and create a feeling of respect and understanding. By confronting conflicts head-on, you show that you're serious about solving problems in a positive and constructive way, which helps you build better relationships with your colleagues.

IMPROVING DIGITAL COMMUNICATION MANNERS

Aiming for a more human and conversational tone, simple things like slow email responses or abrupt sign-offs can cause problems, too. It's a good idea to confirm you've received an email and to set clear expectations on when you'll reply. This not only stops people from getting frustrated but also helps make things fair for everyone. When you're writing an email or message, take a little time to check it for tone and clarity. You want to be sure your message is clear and doesn't have any unintended implications. A well-written message really shows your professionalism and attention to detail.

MAINTAINING PROFESSIONALISM IN CHATS AND INSTANT MESSAGES

Okay, so chats and online messaging are really convenient, but they come with their own set of issues. Because these systems are so informal, it's easy to become too casual in your communication, which may not be right for a workplace. You still need to be respectful, even when you're communicating informally. Watch your tone and language, and avoid using slang or language that could be misunderstood or seem unprofessional. Instead, stick to simple, direct language that respects professional boundaries.

EFFECTIVELY APPLYING HUMOR IN ONLINE COMMUNICATIONS

Humor can be a great way to connect with people and make things more interesting, but you have to be careful when using it online. The Society for Human Resource Management suggests that office humor should be safe and not offend anyone. So, you should stay away from things like religion, politics, and other touchy topics when you're using humor in emails or messages. Be mindful of your audience, and make sure your jokes are respectful and in good taste. A well-placed joke can lighten the mood and help build rapport, but you have to make sure it can't be taken the wrong way or be seen as insensitive.

LET'S GET REAL SCENARIOS

All-Caps Emergency:
You open your inbox to find an email from a coworker with an all-caps subject line screaming urgency, only to discover it's a minor request. Instead of responding in a similar tone, you reply playfully, "Your subject line nearly triggered my emergency response system—can we agree to save all caps for genuine office emergencies?" Your friendly tone encourages clearer email etiquette.

- "My heart just survived your all-caps surprise—let's keep future emails lowercase."
- "Next time, let's save all-caps for actual fires or urgent pizza deliveries."
- "For clarity, could we reserve uppercase for truly urgent matters?"

Emoji Betrayal:
You send a humorous emoji in a chat, only to discover your colleague misinterprets it as sarcasm. You quickly follow up with a friendly message, "Oops, looks like my emoji got lost in translation—just kidding, no sarcasm intended!" Your clear, humorous clarification diffuses tension.

60

- "My emoji seems to have gone rogue—sorry for the confusion!"
- "Did my humor emoji malfunction again? Let me clarify..."
- "I apologize if my message was unclear. Here's what I actually meant..."

Delayed Response Dilemma:

A colleague sends you an email request that you can't respond to immediately. To avoid frustration, you quickly reply, humorously noting, "Just letting you know your message safely arrived—but my inbox is having a busy moment. I'll send a thoughtful reply by end of day!" Your playful note manages expectations clearly.

- "Your email arrived just in time for my afternoon email marathon."
- "Email traffic jam on my side—clearing it shortly!"
- "I've received your request and will respond fully by the end of the day."

Abrupt Sign-Off Surprise:

Your coworker's email ends abruptly, which seems dismissive. Rather than jumping to conclusions, you reply gently and humorously, "Your sign-off threw me off balance—was it shorthand or just an accidental cliffhanger?" Your friendly approach defuses potential misunderstandings.

- "Your sign-off left me with a dramatic cliffhanger!"
- "Your emails end faster than my internet connection on a bad day."
- "I wanted to check in briefly—your email seemed a bit abrupt. Is everything okay?"

Informal Language Lapse:

You realize you've used overly casual language in a client's direct message, possibly appearing unprofessional. Quickly addressing it, you lightly say, "Apologies for that informality slip—my brain briefly entered weekend mode!" Your good-humored acknowledgment restores professionalism smoothly.

- "Looks like my chat went into casual Friday mode—let me clarify."
- "My autocorrect chose informality today. Here's a more professional take!"
- "I apologize for my informal wording earlier—here's a clearer response."

Reply-All Avalanche:

You mistakenly hit "Reply All" and flooded everyone's inbox. To address the mishap, you quickly follow up, "Sorry everyone—my inbox wanted some company and went rogue! No reply necessary." Your good-humored acknowledgment gently reinforces email etiquette.

- "My inbox staged a "Reply All" rebellion—apologies for the digital chaos!"
- "Sorry for triggering an inbox avalanche—the next "Reply All" requires my supervisor's approval."
- "Apologies for the extra messages. I'll be more careful moving forward."

Cryptic Communicator:

You regularly receive unclear messages from a coworker that force you to decode their intent. Instead of getting frustrated, you reply humorously, "Your messages are great brain teasers—any chance we can skip to clarity next time?" Your lighthearted tone gently encourages clearer communication.

- "Are your messages a secret code? I forgot to bring my decoder ring today."
- "Should I call Sherlock to decode your latest note, or could we simplify things?"

- "Clearer messages would help us stay aligned and productive—mind elaborating next time?"

After-Hours Enthusiast:
Your colleague sends non-urgent messages late at night. Instead of responding immediately, you reply the next morning with playful humor, "My phone's strict bedtime kept your message waiting—ready to respond now!" Your upbeat tone gently reinforces personal boundaries. Another great tactic is just not to address the timing of the message since they were likely not expecting a response. Here are some other responses you can try.

- "Late-night messages get put in the digital waiting room until morning."
- "My inbox clocks out earlier than I do—sorry for the delay!"
- "To keep work-life balance healthy, let's handle non-urgent items during office hours."

Here's the thing about online stuff: you've got to be super aware of how your words might land because, let's face it, things can get lost in translation. You've got to think of it like trying to tell a joke over text; sometimes, it just doesn't come across the same.

So, keep it professional, throw in a dash of understanding, and maybe even a sprinkle of grace because, let's be honest, we've all been on the receiving end of a message that made us go, "Huh?" So, just try to be cool about it, and focus on the next thing that matters.

CHAPTER 8 QUIZ: HOW SHOULD YOU HANDLE THESE SCENARIOS?

1. You receive an email from a coworker with an all-caps subject line indicating urgency, only to discover it's a minor request. What's your best response?

2. A colleague misunderstands your humorous emoji in a chat, interpreting it as sarcasm. How should you quickly clarify?

3. You can't immediately respond to a colleague's email request, potentially causing frustration. How can you manage expectations humorously?

4. Your coworker's email ends abruptly, seeming dismissive. How can you address this gently without escalating tensions?

5. You've accidentally sent an overly informal message to a client, possibly appearing unprofessional. How do you address it promptly?

Answers available at the back of the book.

NINE

MANAGING CROSS-GENERATIONAL HUMOR

Okay, imagine this: you're at the office Christmas party trying to connect with people from other departments with a funny joke. But instead, everyone stares at you, confused. Your joke, which you thought was a clever pop culture reference, just didn't land because of the generational gap. The Baby Boomers might smile because they remember it, while the Millennials and Gen Z are looking at each other like, "what?" They probably think your joking needs to #befunny. Humor, like communication, can either connect people or highlight differences you didn't expect.

THE APPLICATION OF HUMOR IN A MULTIGENERATIONAL WORKFORCE

The kind of humor that different generations like—Baby Boomers, Gen X, Millennials, and Gen Z—is often shaped by their life experiences. It's often influenced by the cultural references, politics, and technology they grew up with. For example, Baby Boomers may lean toward more traditional storytelling-type humor, like old sitcoms or stand-up comedy with slow drawn-out punchlines. Their humor often comes from shared experiences, finding the funny in the familiar. Meanwhile,

Gen Z is more into online antics with humor that's chaotic and memes-centered, which often makes older generations shake their heads and wonder what they're even watching.

Humor across generations requires a balance of sensitivity, flexibility, and openness to the unique styles of each age group. Keep in mind the preferences of each generation. In a moment, we'll get into some scenarios that you should be ready to address and how you can address them.

MARKETING FOR GENERATION X THROUGH SARCASM AND SATIRE

Generation X, the often overlooked middle child of the generations, leans heavily into sarcasm and irony. Having come of age during a time of pop culture shifts and political cynicism, they developed a taste for humor that pokes fun at the absurdities of life. It's a bit of rebellious humor, using irony as a tool to expose the flaws of modern society. When engaging with this generation, use a witty and slightly irreverent tone, pushing the boundaries of what is acceptable while recognizing their grit.

CONNECTING WITH MILLENNIALS THROUGH AUTHENTIC AND RELATABLE HUMOR

Millennials, the digital natives straddling the analog and digital worlds, tend to appreciate humor that's fast-paced, relatable, and often shared on social media. For them, humor is a way to connect, creating common ground amidst the chaos of modern life. They often enjoy self-deprecating humor, laughing at the absurdities of adulthood in the world. To connect with Millennials, use humor that feels genuine and universal, reflecting the shared experience of their generation.

USING ABSURDITY AND CREATIVITY TO WIN OVER GENERATION Z

Generation Z's sense of humor is shaped by the endless possibilities of the internet. They tend to enjoy humor that's surreal, ridiculous, and often pulled from viral content, where memes and GIFs are the currency of conversation. For Gen Z, humor is about pushing boundaries and embracing the unconventional. To connect with this generation, use creative and edgy humor (but not too edgy) that's fast-paced.

ESTABLISHING MUTUAL RESPECT AND UNDERSTANDING

Remember, humor, like communication, is very personal and subjective. What one person finds hilarious, another might find irritating or uncomfortable. The key to navigating generational differences in humor is creating an environment where people feel comfortable sharing their sense of humor without fear of being judged or ridiculed. This requires a foundation of mutual respect, where humor brings us together rather than dividing us. By embracing the various humor styles of all generations, you can participate in a workplace where you and your coworkers feel it's okay to use humor to communicate.

GENERATIONAL HUMOR PREFERENCE CHART

Now, let's break down the humor preferences across different generations, highlighting their key characteristics and a few examples:

Generation | Years | Possible Humor Preferences
Baby Boomers (1946 - 1964)

Traditional, narrative-driven humor; examples include classic sitcoms and stand-up comedy

Generation X (1965 - 1980)

> Sarcasm and satire; influenced by pop culture
> and political events

Millennials (1981 - 1996)

> Irony and relatability; quick, witty jokes often
> shared on social media

Generation Z (1997 - 2012)

> Absurd, internet-rooted humor; memes and
> viral content

Use this chart as a reference tool during team discussions on humor preferences, fostering a deeper understanding of each generation's comedic sensibilities.

LET'S GET REAL SCENARIOS

Classic Comedy Conundrum:
You make an '80s sitcom reference at lunch to break the ice. Some older coworkers laugh, but you see puzzled looks from younger teammates. To quickly pivot, you smile at everyone and say, "Maybe my comedy references need updating—what's everyone binge-watching these days?" Your quick adjustment helps bridge generational gaps through shared laughter.

- "Note to self: save retro sitcom jokes for nostalgia night."
- "Looks like my humor has an expiration date—any fresher suggestions?"
- "I'd love to hear everyone's favorite comedies to find common ground."

Meme Misunderstanding:
You share a trending meme during a virtual meeting that your younger coworkers are amused by, but it confuses older colleagues. Quickly noticing the puzzled looks, you lightly clarify, "Sorry, I forgot

memes don't come with subtitles—let me explain!" Your playful explanation creates an inclusive environment for all ages.

- "Memes should really come with age ratings—let me break this down."
- "Next time, I'll attach meme translations for easier viewing."
- "Let me provide context to ensure we're all on the same page."

Sarcasm Slip:
A coworker uses sarcasm during a team brainstorming meeting. This amuses most peers but leaves younger team members uncertain. To smooth things over, you gently joke, "Sarcasm alert—looks like we need an interpreter to translate Gen X humor." Your friendly intervention encourages open dialogue and clearer understanding.

- "Sarcasm just triggered an office-wide buffering moment— allow me to clarify."
- "Sarcasm detected! Initiating translation mode."
- "Let's briefly clarify to ensure everyone is on the same page with our communication."

Viral Video Venture:
Your team hosts a virtual talent show, and generational differences become clear from the contrasting humor styles. Some team members start to heckle humor they don't like. Rather than highlighting the disconnect, you warmly remark, "Comedy has certainly evolved—let's appreciate everyone's unique comedic styles!" Your playful acknowledgment fosters appreciation for diverse forms of humor.

- "Humor diversity check complete—everyone's style is welcome here."
- "Glad we covered comedy across the generations—who says we can't multitask?"
- "Appreciating each other's humor helps strengthen our team's connection."

Irony Insight:

A younger colleague shares a self-deprecating joke during a team meetup, briefly surprising older members unfamiliar with this open style of humor. Recognizing the moment, you gently laugh and say, "Irony alert! For anyone not fluent in Millennial humor, let's unpack that joke together." Your friendly approach invites understanding and sparks inclusive conversation.

- "Caution: irony detected—context loading in 3, 2, 1..."
- "Your honesty just caused a generation-gap hiccup—let's smooth it out."
- "Let's clarify briefly to ensure everyone's comfortable and on board."

Emoji Overload:

Your younger coworker's messages overflow with emojis, confusing older teammates. Rather than letting confusion persist, you jokingly respond, "Your emoji-to-text ratio is record-breaking—any chance we could have fewer pictures and more subtitles next time?" Your humor invites clarity without judgment.

- "Emoji literacy course now open for enrollment."
- "My emoji fluency isn't great—mind throwing in some actual words?"
- "Clearer messaging can ensure everyone understands your intended meaning."

Generational Jargon:

An older colleague uses outdated corporate buzzwords during a meeting, confusing younger staff members. You address it warmly, saying humorously, "Looks like we've hit jargon turbulence—shall we decode these terms for clarity?" Your gentle humor encourages a productive dialogue across generations.

- "Corporate-speak translation service activated—decoding in progress."

- "Let's dust off the jargon dictionary to keep everyone on track."
- "Clear terminology helps everyone follow the discussion effectively."

Pop-Culture Disconnect:
During a casual team chat, you reference a popular '80s movie, leaving younger colleagues visibly puzzled. You notice the disconnect and come back with, "Guess my references just celebrated their retirement—any newer favorites to recommend?" Your cheerful pivot turns confusion into shared laughter and team bonding.

- "Did my movie references go vintage overnight, or am I just classic now?"
- "My pop-culture database needs an update—mind sharing your latest favorites?"
- "Let's find some common cultural references to connect everyone comfortably."

So, the secret sauce for making humor work with everyone, from the intern to the CEO, is basically empathy. Like, put yourself in their shoes. Even if their shoes are totally out of style, you have to be open-minded because what cracks you up might make someone else roll their eyes. Pitching in to create a space where different kinds of humor are cool and respected is like building a workplace where everyone feels included and is in on the joke, especially coworkers across different generations.

Embrace all the different ways people find things funny, and use that to create a workplace that's lively, united, and where everyone feels like they belong—because who doesn't like a good laugh?

CHAPTER 9 QUIZ: HOW SHOULD YOU HANDLE THESE SCENARIOS?

1. You reference a classic sitcom at lunch, amusing older coworkers but confusing younger ones. How can you quickly bridge this generational gap?

2. A trending meme you share delights younger coworkers but leaves older colleagues confused. How do you handle the misunderstanding?

3. During a team brainstorm, sarcasm from an older colleague puzzles younger team members. What's your best move to clarify and ease the tension?

4. At a virtual talent show, diverse generational humor styles emerge clearly. How do you foster appreciation rather than division?

5. Younger colleagues frequently use emojis that older coworkers find confusing. What's a humorous way to encourage clearer communication?

Answers available at the back of the book.

TEN
MANAGING CHANGE & ADDRESSING VOLATILITY

Picture this: you stroll into the office, coffee in hand, ready to tackle the day, when an email pops up with the dreaded subject line: "Organizational changes, please read." Your heart skips a beat, and your mind races with thoughts of restructuring, new job titles, and maybe even the horror of mandatory team-building events that often follow. Welcome to the unpredictable world of organizational change, where uncertainty is the norm and flexibility is your greatest strength.

EMBRACING CHANGE

In business, change is as certain as wanting to sleep on a Monday morning. Whether it's a software update, a merger, or a shifting company strategy, change needs to happen in order for companies to evolve; it's also what's needed for innovation. Let's be honest, managing change can feel like herding cats while juggling flaming torches. It's about balancing productivity, calming employee anxieties, and preventing stress levels from going through the roof. The good news is, with the right strategies, you can navigate these rough waters like a seasoned captain.

EFFECTIVELY NAVIGATING WORKPLACE CHANGES, TRANSITIONS, AND UNCERTAINTY

Managing change at work is both a skill and an art. You will no doubt be on the receiving end of a coworker or two losing their minds because of an upcoming change at work. You are not immune to it either. Change requires a bit of foresight, empathy, and flexibility to transform potentially chaotic situations into opportunities for growth. Effective change management starts with understanding that resistance is a natural human reaction. We're wired to seek stability, so any disruption to the norm can trigger anxiety and uncertainty.

APPLICATION OF HUMAN RESOURCES IN CHANGE MANAGEMENT

Your company's leadership is responsible for guiding your team through any change storms, but sometimes, it doesn't work out so smoothly and there is very little clarity about the rollout of pending changes. According to the paper "Change Management for Human Resources Professionals" by Prosci, it's crucial to align HR with change management processes to overcome challenges like resistance to change, communication breakdowns, and cultural misalignment. However, all too often, the human side of change management is not prioritized, leading to rocky transitions and failed employee buy-in. Recognize that change often brings a sense of loss, whether it's the comfort of a routine, a valued colleague, or a favorite project. So, we'll get into some ways of communicating with your boss when things aren't quite right.

LET'S GET REAL SCENARIOS

Sudden Software Upgrade:
Your team is mid-project when you're suddenly told a new software system will roll out next week. This creates widespread panic. Rather than allowing anxiety to take hold, you calmly joke, "Looks like the tech gods decided we needed a surprise challenge—time for a team

training montage!" Your humorous reassurance motivates your team as you organize training sessions, ensuring everyone transitions smoothly.

- "The software fairy dropped another update—let's decode it together."
- "Who knew our keyboards would need survival training this week?"
- "Let's schedule a training session to ensure everyone feels confident about the new software."

Merger Maze:
A sudden merger announcement creates a lot of uncertainty about team roles and job security. Rather than letting anxiety take over, you lighten the mood by joking, "Welcome to our new corporate reality show—let's skip the drama and go straight to Q&A." Your playful openness eases tension and encourages transparent communication, fostering unity and collaboration.

- "Our merger is like a surprise guest—let's make sure everyone gets acquainted."
- "Is it merger season already? Let's clear the air and get aligned."
- "Regular discussions will help everyone navigate the merger clearly and confidently."

Remote Work Revolution:
When your team suddenly moves to remote work, confusion and isolation start creeping in. Recognizing the importance of connection, you bring up the potential of starting virtual team-building, announcing, "We might be remote, but awkward team-building exercises can still follow us home!" Your playful efforts promote engagement and boost morale despite the distance.

- "Welcome to our pajama-friendly work zone—let's keep connected!"

- "Time to perfect our video-call smiles—daily check-ins start today."
- "Regular virtual meetings will keep our teamwork strong and connected."

Leadership Shuffle:
A key executive abruptly departs, which sends shockwaves throughout the office. Instead of letting anxiety grow, you lightly joke, "Looks like we're playing musical chairs in leadership—let's sit tight and keep dancing." Your calming humor helps ease concerns.

- "Our leadership carousel spins again—let's ensure we all stay steady."
- "Another round of executive musical chairs—grab a seat and let's strategize."
- "Transparent communication will keep everyone informed during this transition."

Policy Overhaul:
New policies are suddenly rolled out and you and your coworkers are overwhelmed. Instead of panicking, you humorously announce, "Policy update incoming—brace yourselves for some exciting reading material! Let's decode it together." Your friendly, humorous approach helps ease stress and promotes understanding through organized discussions and training.

- "Policies got an unexpected reboot—let's unpack them calmly."
- "Surprise: policy makeover! Let's navigate these changes together."
- "Training sessions on new policies will ensure everyone adapts comfortably and clearly."

Talent Turnover:
After several sudden departures, your remaining team feels demoralized and stretched thin with work. Rather than ignoring morale issues,

you cheerfully suggest, "Looks like it's time for a team reboot—how about we support each other through this update?" Your optimistic tone motivates and gets everyone on the same page.

- "Did someone install a revolving door? Let's stabilize things together."
- "Looks like turnover season again—let's strengthen our team bonds."
- "Mentorship programs will help everyone feel supported during transitions."

Office Relocation Surprise:
The company announces an unexpected office move. All of your coworkers are stressing out about the uncertainty. Rather than letting anxiety dominate, you playfully say, "Office relocation adventure ahead! Pack your coffee mugs and your sense of humor—we're on the move." Your upbeat tone transforms anxiety into anticipation.

- "Looks like our desks are taking a field trip—let's pack smartly."
- "Change of scenery incoming! Who's ready for a fresh view?"
- "Clear communication about the move timeline will help everyone adjust smoothly."

Rebranding Rollercoaster:
Your organization abruptly rebrands, and it becomes chaos with your colleagues feeling disoriented. Instead of feeding the confusion, you organize a humorous briefing, joking, "Hold onto your lanyards—we're boarding the rebranding rollercoaster. Let's clarify what this means together." Your friendly approach reduces stress and promotes excitement around the new identity.

- "Our brand just got a makeover—time for a guided tour!"
- "Brand facelift incoming—let's figure out our new look together."

- "Clear explanations about brand changes will keep the team informed and aligned."

Team Restructure Shuffle:
Your team's roles shift dramatically during restructuring, causing confusion. Rather than allowing the backlash of complaints to fester, you host informal chats and humorously announce, "Welcome to 'Who's Who in the New Crew'—let's clear up the cast list!" Your playful yet clear communication helps team members quickly adapt and realign.

- "Role shuffle season—let's get everyone on the same page."
- "Did our job titles just do a dance routine? Time to learn the new choreography."
- "Regular check-ins will clarify roles and help the team stay cohesive."

Let's be real: thriving in any work environment, especially when things are going bonkers, really boils down to how well you handle change. You gotta have empathy—like, try to see where others are coming from, even if they are freaking out about the new coffee machine. Good communication is key, because talking through stuff can help you avoid a *Lord of the Flies* situation at work.

Taking smart steps is like building a team of superheroes who can handle anything that comes their way. Change shouldn't be a road-block; it can actually be a path to new opportunities. So, if you respond the right way, you can turn things that might throw you off into rocket fuel for your growth and success. And who doesn't want to be a rocket?

CHAPTER 10 QUIZ: HOW SHOULD YOU HANDLE THESE SCENARIOS?

1. A sudden software upgrade announcement causes team-wide anxiety mid-project. How do you help your team respond positively?

2. News of a company merger creates uncertainty about job roles and security. How can you lighten the mood and maintain clear communication?

3. Your team abruptly transitions to remote work, causing confusion and isolation. What humorous approach can boost morale and connectivity?

4. A key executive leaves unexpectedly, leading to instability and concern. How can you reassure your team during this uncertainty?

5. A sudden policy overhaul leaves your team overwhelmed and stressed. How do you humorously ease tensions while ensuring understanding?

Answers available at the back of the book.

ELEVEN

WORKPLACE ENVIRONMENT
& PRODUCTIVITY

Ah, the office—it's where big dreams and real ambition meet caffeine. Visions of productivity bump up against the hum of fluorescent lights, and finding the perfect place to work is as impossible as finding a pen with its cap still on. In this chapter, we explore the daily realities of the modern office, a place where the comfort of your space, noise, distractions, cleanliness, and available resources shape our daily work lives. Imagine this: you're at your desk ready to start the day, and suddenly, a coworker's phone call drifts over the wall of the cubicle. It pulls you out of your focus. It's moments like these that show us the office is more than just a place to work. It's a complex ecosystem where productivity and chaos live together in a weird, uneasy balance.

CREATING OPTIMAL WORKSPACE COMFORT

We all dream of finding that perfect workspace because we all want a place that encourages creativity, focus, and teamwork. From ergonomic chairs that promise to hug your lower back like a concerned friend, to carefully placed plants that promise to give us cleaner air, every detail is carefully thought through in our quest for productivity. But even with our best attempts, we'll still have challenges in creating a workspace that works for everyone all the time.

SOLVING REAL-WORLD OFFICE ISSUES, INCLUDING WORKSPACE COMFORT, NOISE, AND DISTRACTIONS

Workspace comfort is about finding that sweet spot where good ergonomics meet your personal style to create a workspace as welcoming as a cozy chair on a rainy day. Sounds nice, right? A tidy and clean workspace is thought to have a real impact on our focus and how much we get done. Work comfort isn't just about your chair; it's about how your desk is set up, the height of your monitor, and the placement of your keyboard. It's about making sure that your workspace feels like an extension of you—a place where you can settle in and be productive.

MANAGING NOISE LEVELS AND WORKPLACE DISTRACTIONS FOR PRODUCTIVITY

How do you deal with the noise at work? Constant noise can really hurt your productivity. Noise can be the background chatter of your coworkers, the hum of office equipment, or even just the occasional bursts of laughter that happen at work. While some people like the hustle and bustle of noise, some need complete silence to be able to focus and get things done. The trick is finding the right balance for you—that sweet spot of noise and silence that meets your own needs. It's not easy.

So, what do you do when it's too noisy for you to work? We'll look at some ways to deal with that in a minute. But other than noise-canceling headphones, one thing to try is to create boundaries within your workspace. Letting people know when you need to focus—a simple sign or closed door—can show that you need uninterrupted time, which will let you get absorbed in your work without constant interruptions.

TAILORING YOUR WORKSPACE TO YOUR NEEDS

Everyone needs to make an efficient office space that works for them because every single person has their own unique needs and wants. What works for someone else might not work for you, and the trick is making your workspace work for your style and needs. When you try to solve real issues like workspace comfort, noise, distractions, tidiness, and resource management, you're building an environment for your well-being and making yourself perform better.

LET'S GET REAL SCENARIOS

Ergonomic Enthusiast:
You've got your ergonomic chair and desk setup perfected, but your workspace remains a chaotic jumble of papers and coffee cups. Coworkers are starting to notice and make jokes, so you humorously announce, "My ergonomic chair asked me nicely to tidy its surroundings—it's feeling lonely in all this clutter." This instantly makes your colleagues aware that you acknowledge their concerns.

- "Turns out my ergonomic chair prefers zen minimalism—time for a desk makeover."
- "My desk chaos has reached legendary status—let's write a tidy sequel."
- "Organizing my workspace will significantly enhance my productivity and clarity."

Noise Navigator:
Your open office setup is always busy, and the constant chatter and ringing phones distract you. Rather than suffering through the noise, you jokingly announce, "Investing in noise-canceling headphones—my new office survival gear." This humorous approach acknowledges distractions openly and helps you focus clearly on tasks.

- "Office noise levels are hitting rock concert status—headphones, here I come!"

- "Found my productivity secret weapon—white noise playlist activated."
- "Noise-canceling headphones have helped me concentrate better in our active workspace."

Distraction Defender:
Social media and casual conversations constantly disrupt your workflow. Instead of giving in, you set clear boundaries by stating to coworkers, "Activating 'do not disturb' mode to avoid getting trapped in the social media abyss—see you on the other side!" Your witty statement signals your need for focus without creating tension.

- "Social media quarantine mode activated—time to get serious."
- "Temporarily muting distractions—catch up with you when I resurface."
- "I'm creating distraction-free zones during work hours to boost productivity."

Cleanliness Crusader:
Though you enjoy the creative chaos on your desk, it starts looking overwhelming and coworkers are starting to notice and comment. Rather than ignoring the comments, you jokingly remark, "Time to rescue my desk from creative chaos—it's begging for some organization therapy." Your humorous acknowledgment encourages you to tidy up, enhancing clarity and efficiency.

- "Desk art installation reaching critical mass—decluttering intervention needed."
- "My sticky-note collection needs a digital upgrade—time to organize!"
- "Maintaining an organized workspace helps me stay creative and productive."

Resource Ruler:
Your outdated equipment struggles to keep up with your project work-

load. Instead of quietly suffering, you lightly approach management and joke, "My computer decided it prefers retirement to upgrades—mind helping me negotiate a tech refresh?" Your humor smoothly initiates a productive discussion on resource improvements.

- "My computer wants to retire early—can we discuss an upgrade?"
- "Think my tech joined the slow-lane club—time for an intervention?"
- "Upgrading our equipment will significantly enhance my ability to deliver effectively."

Temperature Diplomat:
Office temperatures fluctuate wildly, and it usually sparks daily thermostat battles with coworkers. To ease tensions, you humorously remark, "Our thermostat has more drama than reality TV—can we negotiate a peace treaty?" Your playful comment encourages constructive dialogue and comfort compromises.

- "Temperature wars escalating again—time to call for a peace summit."
- "Thermostat negotiations ongoing—let's aim for a temperature UN Assembly."
- "Establishing a comfortable office temperature will help everyone work productively. Let's research what the average office temperature normally is and agree."

Breakroom Battleground:
The shared kitchen consistently devolves into unclean chaos. To inspire a little cooperation, you jokingly mention at the next team meeting, "The breakroom mess is gaining historical status—let's not make future archeologists guess our habits." Your witty nudge encourages better shared-space etiquette without embarrassment.

- "The kitchen sink is resembling abstract art—let's aim for realism."

- "Breakroom mysteries solved: dishes don't clean themselves."
- "Maintaining cleanliness in common areas keeps the workplace pleasant for everyone."

Conference Room Competition:
The most coveted conference room causes regular scheduling conflicts. To defuse frustration, you create a humorous shared calendar titled, "Conference Room Chronicles—let the scheduling games begin!" Your playful framing fosters friendly competition and collaboration.

- "Introducing 'Room Wars'—may the scheduling odds be in your favor!"
- "Welcome to the great conference room reservation rally— please, play nicely!"
- "A shared booking system helps ensure fair and efficient use of our meeting spaces. Let's get a system in place that we all follow."

All right, let's talk about actually getting stuff done. The real key here is keeping productivity up, and that means tackling all the little things that can kill it. We're talking about stuff like: Is your workspace comfy? Is it a zoo in here with all the noise? What about distractions? And seriously, how clean is this place? Plus, having the right tools is also important. So, take control of your workspace because you're the boss of your desk, and don't be afraid to talk to your coworkers about all of these things. You're not being demanding; you're being productive.

CHAPTER 11 QUIZ: HOW SHOULD YOU HANDLE THESE SCENARIOS?

1. Your ergonomic workspace is perfect, but clutter and chaos are taking over. How do you address this openly with colleagues?

2. The constant office chatter and ringing phones are severely impacting your productivity. What humorous approach could you take?

3. Social media notifications and casual office conversations frequently interrupt your workflow. How can you humorously communicate your boundaries?

4. Your outdated computer is slowing down important projects. How do you use humor to initiate a conversation with management?

5. The office thermostat has become a daily source of conflict. How can you humorously ease tensions among coworkers?

Answers available at the back of the book.

TWELVE
REMOTE WORK & VIRTUAL ENVIRONMENT CHALLENGES

I f your daily commute is just a shuffle from your bedroom to your home office, or maybe an artfully arranged laptop on a stack of cookbooks, you're experiencing the reality of remote work. It's where fancy clothes meet pajama pants, and the line between home and office disappears faster than the milk in your coffee. Working in the chaos of your living room can be as unpredictable as getting reliable Wi-Fi at your local coffee shop. In this chapter, we'll talk about the unique challenges of remote work, sharing stories and funny, real-life situations about how to stay professional when your work and home lives mix together.

EMBRACING THE CHAOS OF REMOTE WORK

Working from home is like a perpetual juggling act; every new project or distraction feels like another ball thrown in the air. The mailman and your dog's barking, the refrigerator calling out to you, or social media tempting you to scroll. These distractions can pull even the most focused person away from work. But amidst the chaos, we have the opportunity to rethink how we approach work, create boundaries that protect both our jobs and our personal time, and find new ways to work with others, even when we are working remotely.

MASTERING VIRTUAL MEETINGS, BOUNDARIES, AND PRODUCTIVITY WITH A HEALTHY DOSE OF HUMOR

Remote work etiquette is a tricky thing. It's all about balancing professionalism with the relaxed vibe of working from home. Remember the first time you hopped on a video call only to realize your camera was aimed right at that pile of laundry you swore you'd folded yesterday? Don't worry, you're not alone.

Video calls have their own set of unspoken rules, like having decent lighting and not getting distracted while someone is presenting the quarterly report. Michael Kerr, a speaker from the Canadian Business Hall of Fame, suggests making a fun video call etiquette guide to help navigate these situations. This guide could include both serious suggestions, like muting your phone and closing extra tabs, and silly ones, like introducing the pets who always make a cameo in your video.

ENHANCING ENGAGEMENT IN VIRTUAL MEETINGS

Virtual meetings, a key part of working remotely, have their own challenges. Without being in the same room, it's easy for people to get distracted or feel disconnected. It's way too simple to start checking email or scrolling through social media while someone's giving a presentation. To avoid this, video call etiquette is really important. Simple things like muting your mic when you're not talking, looking at the camera, and using the chat for questions can turn a messy call into a useful discussion. But all of this depends on whether your internet decides to work. There's nothing more frustrating than getting ready to explain something crucial, and then, your screen freezes, leaving you in an awkward still frame.

ESTABLISHING EFFECTIVE BOUNDARIES FOR WORK-LIFE BALANCE

Setting boundaries is key when you work remotely. When your office is just steps from your living room, it's hard to switch off at the end of the day. The temptation to answer one more email or finish that last report after dinner can make the workday never-ending.

To keep a healthy balance between work and life, try to have a dedicated workspace separate from your living area. This physical separation helps your brain understand that when you're in that space, it's work time, and when you leave it, it's time to relax and spend time with friends and family. Also, try setting specific work hours and sharing them with your coworkers, so that everyone knows what to expect.

Even with its difficulties, remote work can give you flexibility, letting you design your workday around your lifestyle and what you prefer. No matter what approach you choose, just remember that remote work is not a one-size-fits-all solution. Here are some ideas to deal with the challenges you might face.

LET'S GET REAL SCENARIOS

Virtual Background Blunder:
You're on an important video call when your beautiful virtual background glitches, revealing the messy room behind you. Instead of panicking, you laugh and say, "Looks like virtual reality just collided with my actual reality—bonus points if you spot the laundry pile!" Your playful honesty transforms embarrassment into a fun bonding moment.

- "Virtual backgrounds: keeping our laundry secrets since 2020."

- "Today's video call is sponsored by my messy home office!"
- "Apologies for the visual distraction; let's get back on track."

Productivity Pro:

Working from home has made staying focused a challenge, so you decide to test out the Pomodoro Technique, the productivity method of working in short, focused periods (usually 25 minutes) with short breaks to improve concentration. You humorously announce to coworkers, "I've officially upgraded my work routine to tomatoes—productivity just got juicy!" The playful acknowledgment helps you stick to intervals of focused work and rewarding breaks.

- "Just mastered the art of working in tomato-sized bursts."
- "Pomodoro sessions in progress—please hold distractions until my next tomato break."
- "Using timed intervals has significantly boosted my productivity."

In-House Boundary Builder:

Your family treats your presence at home as an open invitation for errands and interruptions. Rather than getting annoyed by the expectations, you gently joke, "Attention household: my home office is now a no-fly zone between 9 and 5—please schedule visits accordingly." Your humorous tone effectively communicates your work hours and establishes clear boundaries.

- "Family hotline closed for business hours—normal service resumes after 5 PM."
- "Now taking reservations for family interruptions—after office hours only."
- "Establishing clear work hours helps maintain my productivity and work-life balance."

Humor Hero:

Remote work feels isolating, so you inject a little humor into daily interactions. You regularly share amusing memes and playful emails, like, "Just doing my part so social distancing doesn't become social dullness!" Your light-hearted communications boost team morale and maintain a positive remote-work atmosphere.

- "Today's agenda: humor delivery to all remote offices."
- "Socially distant, humorously connected."
- "Using humor helps our team stay engaged and connected remotely."

Focused Freelancer:
Struggling with distractions, you invest in noise-canceling headphones and app blockers to create a focused workspace. You jokingly tell your colleagues, "Activating fortress of solitude mode—disturbances temporarily blocked." Your playful yet clear boundary-setting approach noticeably improves your efficiency.

- "Distraction shields up—let productivity commence."
- "Just upgraded my workspace to distraction-proof status."
- "Creating a focused workspace helps me deliver high-quality work consistently."

Time-Zone Tango:
Scheduling meetings across global time zones feels nearly impossible, which is causing frustration. To lighten the mood, you joke during the next virtual team call, "These time zones have me feeling like a confused time traveler—someone passes the coffee and reminds me what year it is!" Your humorous approach alleviates scheduling tension.

- "Today's meeting is brought to you by coffee and jet lag."
- "Navigating time zones like a professional clock-spinner."
- "Clear scheduling helps us collaborate effectively across global time zones."

Accidental Screen Share:
A new company hire accidentally shares their cluttered desktop during

a virtual meeting. Quickly defusing potential embarrassment, you warmly joke, "Looks like your screen decided to give us a behind-the-scenes tour—need a moment to sweep the digital floor?" Your friendly humor eases tension and helps your teammate feel comfortable.

- "Your desktop just volunteered for show-and-tell—thanks for the transparency!"
- "Bonus points awarded for bravery in screen-sharing today."
- "No worries, we've all been there—let's take a quick pause if you'd like."

Mute Button Mishap:
You had the dreaded mute button selected for the first five minutes of your presentation, and you didn't notice people trying to get your attention. Laughing it off, you quickly recover with, "And that concludes the silent movie portion—here comes the talkie version!" Your cheerful humor puts everyone at ease and smoothly restarts your presentation.

- "Just delivered a compelling speech—too bad it was mime-only."
- "Unmuting now for your listening pleasure!"
- "Apologies, let's rewind—I was muted. Here's what I intended to share."

One of the most challenging aspects of remote work is deciding whether or not to put on pants. On the one hand, your coworkers will only see you from the waist up, and who are they to judge your choice of pajama bottoms? On the other hand, you might actually need to get the mail that day, so, decisions, decisions. But remote work isn't just about figuring out your attire. It's about challenging the traditional ideas of what it means to be productive, connected, and happy—all while resisting the urge to work from the comfort of your bed. Don't be that person who's working part-time while collecting a full-time check. Trust, everyone notices.

CHAPTER 12 QUIZ: HOW SHOULD YOU HANDLE THESE SCENARIOS?

1. Your virtual background suddenly fails, revealing your messy room during an important video call. How do you respond?

2. You're struggling to stay focused while working remotely, frequently tempted by distractions. How do you address this?

3. Your family keeps interrupting your workday at home, unaware of your professional boundaries. What can you say?

4. Remote team meetings frequently feel chaotic and distracting. How do you introduce effective meeting etiquette?

5. Time zone differences make scheduling virtual meetings feel nearly impossible. How do you alleviate the tension?

Answers available at the back of the book.

THIRTEEN
HR-APPROVED SKILLS IN ACTION

RECOMMENDED RESPONSE TONE (ALL SCENARIOS)

This section outlines recommended response tones for various workplace scenarios. We'll walk through each scenario, its recommended response tone, and an example quote that demonstrates that tone.

Recommended Response Tone

Playful Humor

Scenario Example | Example Quote
Virtual Background Blunder

"Looks like my virtual reality just collided with actual reality—bonus points if you spot the laundry pile!"

Accidental Screen Share

"Looks like your screen is giving us a behind-the-scenes tour—need a moment?"

Reply-All Avalanche

"My inbox wanted some company and went rogue!"

Mute Button Mishap

"And that concludes the silent movie portion—here comes the talkie version!"

Emoji Misunderstanding

"My emoji seems to have gone rogue—sorry for the confusion!"

Ergonomic Enthusiast

"My ergonomic chair asked nicely to tidy its surroundings—it's lonely in clutter."

Temperature Diplomat

"Our thermostat negotiations rival international diplomacy—time for a truce?"

Recommended Response Tone	Scenario Example	Example Quote
Humorous & Direct	Chronic Procrastinator	"Your deadlines seem optional—can we set some firmer ones?"
	Blame Shifter	"Our project tracker ensures everyone's contributions shine."
	Corner-Cutter	"Your speed is impressive—but let's not leave quality behind."
	Credit Hog	"Loved your presentation—maybe next time we co-present?"
	Boundary Pusher	"My inbox practices strict bedtime—even if I don't always follow suit."
	Numbers Game	"Looks like our numbers started creative writing—let's stick to nonfiction."

Recommended Response Tone

Humorous & Direct

Scenario Example | Example Quote
Chronic Procrastinator

"Your deadlines seem optional—can we set some firmer ones?"

Blame Shifter

"Our project tracker ensures everyone's contributions shine."

Corner-Cutter

"Your speed is impressive—but let's not leave quality behind."

Credit Hog

"Loved your presentation—maybe next time we co-present?"

Boundary Pusher

"My inbox practices strict bedtime—even if I don't always follow suit."

Numbers Game

"Looks like our numbers started creative writing—let's stick to nonfiction."

Recommended Response Tone	Scenario Example	Example Quote
Gentle Humor	Serial Interrupter	"Our meetings aren't karaoke—mind letting me finish my solo?"
	Overbearing Office Mate	"Should I start selling tickets, or can we establish a 'no-fly' zone?"
	Boundary-Crossing Screen Watcher	"Should I sell tickets, or could we respect my screen privacy?"
	Hovering Hawk	"Thinking of pulling up a chair, or can we set regular check-ins instead?"

Recommended Response Tone

Gentle Humor

Scenario Example | Example Quote
Serial Interrupter

"Our meetings aren't karaoke—mind letting me finish my solo?"

Overbearing Office Mate

"Should I start selling tickets, or can we establish a 'no-fly' zone?"

Boundary-Crossing Screen Watcher

"Should I sell tickets, or could we respect my screen privacy?"

Hovering Hawk

"Thinking of pulling up a chair, or can we set regular check-ins instead?"

Recommended Response Tone	Scenario Example	Example Quote
Friendly & Warm	Meme Misunderstanding	"Sorry, I forgot memes don't come with subtitles—let me explain!"
	Classic Comedy Conundrum	"Maybe my comedy references need updating—what's everyone watching?"
	Pop-Culture Disconnect	"Guess my references just celebrated retirement—any newer favorites?"
	Inappropriate Jokester	"Careful—your jokes might soon star in an HR training video."

Recommended Response Tone

Friendly & Warm

Scenario Example | Example Quote
Meme Misunderstanding

"Sorry, I forgot memes don't come with subtitles—let me explain!"

Classic Comedy Conundrum

"Maybe my comedy references need updating—what's everyone watching?"

Pop-Culture Disconnect

"Guess my references just celebrated retirement—any newer favorites?"

Inappropriate Jokester

"Careful—your jokes might soon star in an HR training video."

Recommended Response Tone	Scenario Example	Example Quote
Professional & Clear	Informal Language Lapse	"I apologize for my informal wording earlier. Here's a clearer response."
	Numbers Game	"Integrity in reporting is crucial for our credibility."
	Expense-Report Magician	"Accuracy in reporting expenses helps maintain our integrity."

Recommended Response Tone

Professional & Clear

Scenario Example | Example Quote
Informal Language Lapse

"I apologize for my informal wording earlier. Here's a clearer response."

Numbers Game

"Integrity in reporting is crucial for our credibility."

Expense-Report Magician

"Accuracy in reporting expenses helps maintain our integrity."

Recommended Response Tone	Scenario Example	Example Quote
Calmly Reassuring	Merger Maze	"Welcome to our new corporate reality show—let's clear things up."
	Sudden Software Upgrade	"Looks like the tech gods sent us a challenge—time for a team training montage!"
	Office Relocation Surprise	"Office relocation ahead—pack your mugs and humor, we're moving!"
	Leadership Shuffle	"Looks like musical chairs in leadership—let's stay calm and steady."

Recommended Response Tone

Calmly Reassuring

Scenario Example | Example Quote
Merger Maze

"Welcome to our new corporate reality show—let's clear things up."

Sudden Software Upgrade

"Looks like the tech gods sent us a challenge—time for a team training montage!"

Office Relocation Surprise

"Office relocation ahead—pack your mugs and humor, we're moving!"

Leadership Shuffle

"Looks like musical chairs in leadership—let's stay calm and steady."

Recommended Response Tone	Scenario Example	Example Quote
Clear Boundary-Setting	After-Hours Texter	"To keep work-life balance, handle non-urgent matters during office hours."
	After-Hours Enthusiast	"My notifications follow strict bedtime—happy to reply now."
	Breakroom Battleground	"Our kitchen dreams of cleanliness—let's make that happen."

Recommended Response Tone

Clear Boundary-Setting

Scenario Example | Example Quote

After-Hours Texter

"To keep work-life balance, handle non-urgent matters during office hours."

After-Hours Enthusiast

"My notifications follow strict bedtime—happy to reply now."

Breakroom Battleground

"Our kitchen dreams of cleanliness—let's make that happen."

SCENARIO OUTCOMES & GOALS TABLE:

This section presents workplace scenarios organized by the outcome you want to achieve—like setting boundaries, improving communication, or boosting morale. For each one, we'll walk through the goal, a few example scenarios, and recommended responses you can try.

Desired Outcome	Scenario Examples	Recommended Responses (Quotes)
Establish Clear Boundaries	After-Hours Texter After-Hours Enthusiast Boundary Pusher	"My inbox sleeps early—let's handle it tomorrow." "Notifications follow strict bedtime—let's catch up now." "My inbox clocks out promptly at five."
Enhance Team Morale	Virtual Background Blunder Emoji Misunderstanding Rebranding Rollercoaster	"Bonus points if you spot my laundry pile!" "My emoji seems rogue—sorry for confusion!" "Hold onto your lanyards—let's navigate this rebranding together!"
Encourage Accountability	Blame Shifter Chronic Procrastinator Corner-Cutter	"Project tracking tool keeps everyone accountable." "Deadlines seem optional—let's set firmer ones." "Your speed is impressive, let's keep quality high."

Improve Communication	Email Avalanche	"Can we align this avalanche into a single clear message?"
	Reply-All Avalanche	
	Abrupt Sign-Off Surprise	"Inbox wanted some company—apologies for the chaos!"
		"Your sign-off threw me off—can we clarify?"
Encourage Transparency	Credit Hog	"Loved your presentation—maybe next time we co-present?"
	Numbers Game	
	Expense-Report Magician	"Numbers started creative writing—returning to nonfiction."
		"Receipts are getting creative—time to check policy."
Reduce Tension & Anxiety	Merger Maze	"Welcome to the merger—let clear things up."
	Sudden Software Upgrade	
	Office Relocation Surprise	"Tech gods sent a challenge—training montage!"
		"Relocation ahead—pack humor, we're moving!"
Clarify Expectations	Job Description Mystery	"This job feels like choose-your-adventure—mind clarifying?"
	Role Riddle	
	Goalpost Mover	"This role seems unclear—help me find the right page?"
		"The goals are wandering—can we anchor them?"

SCENARIO-ACTION STEPS TABLE:

This section outlines scenario action steps for various workplace situations. Let's walk through each scenario. I'll share a short description, the immediate action you can take, a follow-up action, and finally, a recommended quote that you can use for that scenario.

Scenario Title	Short Description	Step 1 (Immediate Action)	Step 2 (Follow-up Action)	Recommended Quote
Accidental Screen Share	Coworker unintentionally shares messy screen	Address gently with humor	Pause briefly for privacy	"Your screen decided to share secrets—need a sec?"
Promotion Puzzle	Passed over for promotion unexpectedly	Schedule feedback meeting	Clarify improvement areas	"My promotion got lost—can we track it down?"
Chronic Procrastinator	Coworker consistently misses deadlines	Arrange a casual check-in	Address concerns openly	"Deadlines seem optional—let's set firmer ones."
Mute Button Mishap	Mic muted on a call unknowingly	Lighten moment with humor	Clearly restart presentation	"Just concluded this silent movie—now for the talkie version!"
Credit Collector	Boss takes credit for your work	Approach boss privately	Provide evidence gently	"Loved your summary—may be next time we co-present?"
Emoji Misunderstanding	Joke misunderstood in chat	Clarify intent humorously	Explain briefly for clarity	"My emoji went rogue—sorry for the confusion!"

Accidental Screen Share

Coworker unintentionally shares messy screen

Address gently with humor

Pause briefly for privacy

"Your screen decided to share secrets—need a sec?"

Promotion Puzzle

Passed over for promotion unexpectedly

Schedule feedback meeting

Clarify improvement areas

"My promotion got lost—can we track it down?"

. . .

103

Chronic Procrastinator

Coworker consistently misses deadlines

Arrange a casual check-in

Address concerns openly

"Deadlines seem optional—let's set firmer ones."

Mute Button Mishap

Mic muted on a call unknowingly

Lighten moment with humor

Clearly restart presentation

"Just concluded this silent movie—now for the talkie version!"

Credit Collector

Boss takes credit for your work

Approach boss privately

Provide evidence gently

"Loved your summary—maybe next time we co-present?"

Emoji Misunderstanding

Joke misunderstood in chat

Clarify intent humorously

Explain briefly for clarity

"My emoji went rogue—sorry for the confusion!"

Corner-Cutter

Coworker sacrifices quality for speed

Document & address privately

Support for quality improvement

"Your speed is impressive, but don't sacrifice quality."

Reply-All Avalanche

Accidentally replying all unnecessarily
Quickly acknowledge humorously
Gently remind of email etiquette
"Inbox went rogue—apologies for the digital chaos!"

Informal Language Lapse

Casual language used unintentionally
Apologize and clarify professionally
Reassure professionalism
"Apologies for my informality—here's clearer wording."

Blame Shifter

Coworker avoids responsibility
Suggest using project tracker
Encourage accountability
"Our tracker keeps everyone's contributions clear."

Leadership Shuffle

Key executive unexpectedly leaves
Reassure calmly and transparently
Outline next steps clearly
"Leadership musical chairs—let's stay calm and steady."

Boundary Pusher

Coworker repeatedly tests boundaries
Reinforce boundaries humorously
Reiterate clearly later
"Inbox practices bedtime—even if I forget."

FOURTEEN
QUIZ RESULTS

Welcome to the Quiz Results section of the book. This is your chance to test how well you've absorbed the concepts from each chapter—and see how your instincts line up with HR-approved communication strategies.

At the end of each chapter, you read five scenario-based quiz questions. Now, as promised, this section brings them all together—both the questions and their suggested responses. We'll start by presenting all five questions from the chapter so you can take a moment to reflect on how you'd handle each one.

Then, we'll follow up with a recommended response for each question. Of course, as you learned throughout the book, there are several ways to handle different scenarios, but these responses give you a quick way to challenge yourself with the key takeaways from this book and to provide an HR-approved way to address different scenarios.

Think of this as your back-of-the-book bonus—designed to help you reflect, reinforce key communication takeaways, and sharpen your workplace communication skills.

CHAPTER 1 QUIZ: HOW SHOULD YOU HANDLE THESE SCENARIOS?

1. You receive a memo from your manager that is so vague it feels like a puzzle. What's your best approach?

2. Your inbox is flooded with contradictory emails from multiple coworkers. How should you manage this confusion?

3. A coworker unintentionally makes an insensitive remark during a meeting, causing discomfort. What's the appropriate next step?

4. Two departments are arguing fiercely about resource allocation. How can you ease this tension?

5. Language barriers with an international team are causing project confusion. What's a good way to address this?

Chapter 1 Suggested Quiz Responses:

1. "Appreciate the creative briefing, but could we quickly translate this into plain English for clarity's sake?"

2. "Looks like we have a lot of perspectives—I vote for less inbox ping-pong and a quick video huddle to align."

3. "Your comment landed differently than I think you intended. Can we briefly unpack it together?"

4. "We've got competing priorities doing their best impressions of emergencies. Shall we sort them calmly together?"

5. "We might have accidentally invented a new language between us. Shall we decode it together?"

CHAPTER 2 QUIZ: HOW SHOULD YOU HANDLE THESE SCENARIOS?

1. Your coworker treats deadlines as flexible suggestions, leaving tasks unfinished until the last minute. How do you humorously yet constructively address their procrastination?

2. A colleague frequently avoids responsibility during meetings and shifts blame elsewhere. What's a humorous way to encourage account-ability?

3. A team member consistently disappears when workloads become heavy, causing frustration. How can you lightly address their absence?

4. Your coworker struggles regularly with specific tasks, affecting overall performance. What's a friendly yet helpful way to approach them?

5. A teammate regularly rushes tasks, resulting in frequent errors. How do you gently and humorously suggest focusing more on quality?

Chapter 2 Suggested Quiz Responses:

1. "Your deadlines seem to enjoy scenic detours—want help creating a roadmap to the finish line?"

2. "We need a tool that helps ensure credit and blame get distributed equally—it's democracy, workplace-style!"

3. "Your disappearing acts are impressive—but we need your starring role for the whole show."

4. "Looks like this task is giving you a tough time—want to tag-team it or call in backup?"

5. "Your drafts have great suspense—I never know which errors I'll find next! Want help making it less thrilling for everyone?"

CHAPTER 3 QUIZ: HOW SHOULD YOU HANDLE THESE SCENARIOS?

1. Your coworker frequently leans over your workspace to critique your desktop or emails. What's a humorous way to gently communicate your need for personal space?

2. A colleague repeatedly interrupts you during meetings. How can you humorously encourage them to allow you to finish speaking?

3. Your coworker begins sharing workplace rumors again. What's a friendly yet clear way to discourage office gossip?

4. A team member consistently makes inappropriate jokes during meetings. What's a playful yet firm way to encourage appropriate humor?

5. Your supervisor often sends late-night work messages. How can you humorously reinforce healthy work-life boundaries?

Chapter 3 Suggested Quiz Responses:

1. "Should I start charging rent for desk visits, or can we agree on some space boundaries?"

2. "Our conversations are turning into duets—can I finish my solo first?"

3. "Thanks, but I canceled my subscription to workplace gossip."

4. "Careful, HR might ask you to guest-star in their next training video."

5. "Looks like your message arrived after my work-life boundaries kicked in."

CHAPTER 4 QUIZ: HOW SHOULD YOU HANDLE THESE SCENARIOS?

1. Your coworker constantly highlights flaws in every initiative, dampening team enthusiasm. How can you gently address their persistent negativity with humor?

2. A colleague regularly spreads office gossip, causing unnecessary tension. How do you humorously redirect the conversation toward factual information?

3. A senior coworker often uses aggressive tactics that intimidate others. What's an assertive yet humorous way to encourage respectful collaboration?

4. Your coworker consistently delivers subtle insults disguised as compliments. How can you humorously request clearer, more direct communication?

5. A team member habitually complains about everything from snacks to room temperature. How can you humorously encourage them to provide constructive solutions instead?

Chapter 4 Suggested Quiz Responses:

1. "If pessimism were an Olympic sport, you'd be undefeated—can you help us score some positivity points?"

2. "Our office drama could win Daytime Emmys— how about we save spoilers and stick to facts?"

3. "I didn't realize intimidation was on today's meeting agenda—let's try collaboration instead."

4. "I admire your skill in compliments—you always keep us guessing. Mind aiming giving your critique straight next time?"

5. "Your complaint skills are unmatched. Ready to switch sides and champion solutions so we can experience what you have in mind?"

CHAPTER 5 QUIZ: HOW SHOULD YOU HANDLE THESE SCENARIOS?

1. A coworker presents your hard work as their own during a team meeting. How can you address this privately with a bit of humor?

2. Your coworker regularly takes your privately shared ideas and publicly claims credit. What's a humorous yet clear way to address this issue?

3. Your manager clearly favors one employee, affecting team morale. How can you humorously encourage transparency around opportunities?

4. A colleague frequently sacrifices quality to meet deadlines, putting the team's reputation at risk. How can you gently address this concern with humor?

5. You discover colleagues manipulating financial numbers to hit targets. What's a humorous yet serious approach to address this ethically?

Chapter 5 Suggested Quiz Responses:

1. "I loved your presentation—probably because it sounded exactly like the notes I wrote last week. Maybe we can collaborate openly next time?"

2. "It seems we're sharing a creative wavelength again—maybe next time we should discuss and present our ideas together?"

3. "Seems there might be a VIP list for special assignments—any chance we could make the criteria public, so everyone gets a shot?"

4. "I appreciate speed, but let's avoid the 'fix-it-later' method—it's getting a bit too thrilling."

5. "Looks like our numbers took up creative writing—let's get back to nonfiction."

CHAPTER 6 QUIZ: HOW SHOULD YOU HANDLE THESE SCENARIOS?

1. Your boss frequently hovers over your workspace, closely watching your every move. How can you humorously advocate for more autonomy?

2. During meetings, your boss often takes credit for your ideas. How can you politely and playfully address this issue?

3. Your supervisor insists on controlling every detail, making you feel micromanaged. What humorous approach could you use to suggest more independence?

4. Your manager consistently points out flaws without providing helpful suggestions. How can you gently encourage more constructive feedback?

5. Your manager frequently changes project goals mid-stream, causing confusion. How can you address this issue humorously and effectively?

Chapter 6 Suggested Quiz Responses:

1. "Thinking of pulling up a chair, or can we set regular check-ins instead?"

2. "Loved your summary of my work—next time, I would love to be involved to co-present and make it official."

3. "Maybe it's time we cut the puppet strings—think I could audition for a solo act on the next project?"

4. "I see my work inspired another round of commentary; I appreciate your sharp insights—any chance we pair your critiques with some actionable tips so I can ace the next round?

5. "Our project goals seem to have commitment issues—how do we can help them settle down this time?"

CHAPTER 7 QUIZ: HOW SHOULD YOU HANDLE THESE SCENARIOS?

1. You discover your name missing from the promotion list despite strong performances. How can you address this positively with your manager?

2. Your assigned tasks keep changing unexpectedly, leaving you confused about your responsibilities. What's a humorous way to clarify your role?

3. Your innovative contributions consistently go unnoticed by leadership. How do you gently bring attention to your efforts?

4. You realize your limited internal network might be affecting your career growth. How can you humorously approach colleagues to expand your connections?

5. You've repeatedly exceeded expectations, yet recognition remains elusive. How can you playfully initiate a conversation about receiving acknowledgment?

Chapter 7 Suggested Quiz Responses:

1. "Seems my promotion took a detour—can we discuss the roadmap so I know how to reach my destination next time?"

2. "My job description feels like a mystery novel lately—can we clarify the plot?"

3. "I think my contributions turned invisible again—mind helping me make them visible?"

4. "Turns out my network is smaller than my Wi-Fi range—care to help me expand coverage?"

5. "I think my achievements might be stuck in stealth mode again—could we discuss how to make sure they're more visible moving forward?"

CHAPTER 8 QUIZ: HOW SHOULD YOU HANDLE THESE SCENARIOS?

1. You receive an email from a coworker with an all-caps subject line indicating urgency, only to discover it's a minor request. What's your best response?

2. A colleague misunderstands your humorous emoji in a chat, interpreting it as sarcasm. How should you quickly clarify?

3. You can't immediately respond to a colleague's email request, potentially causing frustration. How can you manage expectations humorously?

4. Your coworker's email ends abruptly, seeming dismissive. How can you address this gently without escalating tensions?

5. You've accidentally sent an overly informal message to a client, possibly appearing unprofessional. How do you address it promptly?

Chapter 8 Suggested Quiz Responses:

1. "Your subject line nearly triggered my emergency response system—can we agree to save all caps for genuine office emergencies?"

2. "Oops, looks like my emoji got lost in translation—just kidding, no sarcasm intended!"

3. "Just letting you know your message safely arrived—but my inbox is having a busy moment. I'll send a thoughtful reply by end of day!"

4. "Your sign-off threw me off balance—was it shorthand or just an accidental cliffhanger?"

5. "Apologies for that informality slip—my brain briefly entered weekend mode!"

CHAPTER 9 QUIZ: HOW SHOULD YOU HANDLE THESE SCENARIOS?

1. You reference a classic sitcom at lunch, amusing older coworkers but confusing younger ones. How can you quickly bridge this generational gap?

2. A trending meme you share delights younger coworkers but leaves older colleagues confused. How do you handle the misunderstanding?

3. During a team brainstorm, sarcasm from an older colleague puzzles younger team members. What's your best move to clarify and ease the tension?

4. At a virtual talent show, diverse generational humor styles emerge clearly. How do you foster appreciation rather than division?

5. Younger colleagues frequently use emojis that older coworkers find confusing. What's a humorous way to encourage clearer communication?

Chapter 9 Suggested Quiz Responses:

1. "Maybe my comedy references need updating—what's everyone binge-watching these days?"

2. "Sorry, I forgot memes don't come with subtitles—let me explain!"

3. "Sarcasm alert—looks like we need an interpreter to translate Gen-to-Gen humor."

4. "Comedy has certainly evolved—let's appreciate everyone's unique comedic styles!"

5. "Your emoji-to-text ratio is record-breaking—any chance we could have fewer pictures and more subtitles next time?"

CHAPTER 10 QUIZ: HOW SHOULD YOU HANDLE THESE SCENARIOS?

1. A sudden software upgrade announcement causes team-wide anxiety mid-project. How do you help your team respond positively?

2. News of a company merger creates uncertainty about job roles and security. How can you lighten the mood and maintain clear communication?

3. Your team abruptly transitions to remote work, causing confusion and isolation. What humorous approach can boost morale and connectivity?

4. A key executive leaves unexpectedly, leading to instability and concern. How can you reassure your team during this uncertainty?

5. A sudden policy overhaul leaves your team overwhelmed and stressed. How do you humorously ease tensions while ensuring understanding?

Chapter 10 Suggested Quiz Responses:

1. "Looks like the tech gods decided we needed a surprise challenge—time for a team training montage!"

2. "Welcome to our new corporate reality show—let's skip the drama and go straight to Q&A."

3. "We might be remote, but awkward team-building exercises can still follow us home!"

4. "Looks like we're playing musical chairs in leadership—let's sit tight and keep dancing."

5. "Policy update incoming—brace yourselves for some exciting reading material! Let's decode it together."

CHAPTER 11 QUIZ: HOW SHOULD YOU HANDLE THESE SCENARIOS?

1. Your ergonomic workspace is perfect, but clutter and chaos are taking over. How do you address this openly with colleagues?

2. The constant office chatter and ringing phones are severely impacting your productivity. What humorous approach could you take?

3. Social media notifications and casual office conversations frequently interrupt your workflow. How can you humorously communicate your boundaries?

4. Your outdated computer is slowing down important projects. How do you use humor to initiate a conversation with management?

5. The office thermostat has become a daily source of conflict. How can you humorously ease tensions among coworkers?

Chapter 11 Suggested Quiz Responses:

1. "My ergonomic chair asked me nicely to tidy its surroundings—it's feeling lonely in all this clutter."

2. "Office noise levels are hitting rock concert status—headphones, here I come!"

3. "Activating 'do not disturb' mode to avoid getting trapped in the social media abyss—see you on the other side!"

4. "My computer decided it prefers retirement to upgrades—mind helping me negotiate a tech refresh?"

5. "Our thermostat has more drama than reality TV—can we negotiate a peace treaty?"

CHAPTER 12 QUIZ: HOW SHOULD YOU HANDLE THESE SCENARIOS?

1. Your virtual background suddenly fails, revealing your messy room during an important video call. How do you respond?
2. You're struggling to stay focused while working remotely, frequently tempted by distractions. How do you address this?
3. Your family keeps interrupting your workday at home, unaware of your professional boundaries. What can you say?
4. Remote team meetings frequently feel chaotic and distracting. How do you introduce effective meeting etiquette?
5. Time zone differences make scheduling virtual meetings feel nearly impossible. How do you alleviate the tension?

Chapter 12 Suggested Quiz Responses:
 1. Laugh and say, "Looks like virtual reality just collided with my actual reality—bonus points if you spot the laundry pile!"
 2. Humorously announce to coworkers, "I've officially upgraded my work routine to tomatoes—productivity just got juicy!"
 3. Playfully inform your family, "Family hotline closed for business hours—normal service resumes after 5 PM."
 4. Create a humorous video meeting etiquette guide that combines serious tips ("mute your mic when not speaking") with playful suggestions ("introduce wandering pets!").
 5. Lighten the mood by joking, "These time zones have me feeling like a confused time traveler—someone passes the coffee and reminds me what year it is!"

CONCLUSION

Throughout this book, we've explored the real-world challenges that can pop up in any workplace. We've learned how to use humor to make important points to coworkers, ease tension, and relieve stress. This book is all about giving you over 500 HR-approved ways to express how you feel without stepping on toes—and creating a much better work environment for you.

It's about helping you use humor wisely in your daily work. So, if you've ever wanted to tell your coworkers what you really thought, but you also wanted to keep your job, you now have a toolbox of strategies you can use. Think of this guide as your cheat sheet for HR-approved conversations. Whether you've rolled your eyes at endless communication fails or obnoxious behaviors from certain office mates, this book was written with you in mind.

We've learned how to address behaviors that are inefficient, confusing, repetitive, or just plain weird, all without causing conflict. We've taken on the tough topics of toxic behaviors and negative attitudes armed with a bit of humor and positivity. We've looked into the details of ethics and professionalism, always remembering that humor should be respectful and honest. We've also explored how to handle humor across different generations, appreciating that everything is not for everyone.

Remember, the goal isn't to become a comedian or force humor into every situation. It's about knowing when and how to use humor intentionally, always being professional and appropriate. By using humor thoughtfully, you can create a more positive and productive work environment for yourself and your colleagues. The real magic happens when you put these ideas into action. Start small with a lighthearted comment or a funny story to ease tension and see how well-placed humor can change your workday. It can strengthen your professional relationships and turn frustrating situations into opportunities for connection.

As we wrap up this book, I'd like to thank you for your dedication to improving your workplace interactions through humor. By embracing laughter, you're not just improving your own experience, but also contributing to a more fun and engaging workplace for everyone around you. Thanks for joining me on this journey.

I wish you the best as you continue to explore the wonderful world of workplace humor.

CLOSING THOUGHTS: A FINAL NOTE

You made it! By reaching this point, you've shown you're ready to take action, think collaboratively, and reduce your own workplace stressors. Now, I have one last request: can you help pay it forward?

Would you be so kind as to scan the QR code to leave a quick review? It will take less than 2-3 minutes. You can scan the QR code below to leave a review.

Your feedback not only helps me improve future resources, but also fuels others like you on their journey to cope with workplace challenges without landing themselves in trouble.

Also, visit HRapprovedways.com to access the review page and bonus content.

Keep connecting!

OVER 500 HR APPROVED WAYS TO SAY (ALMOST) ANYTHING TO COWORKERS

Now that you've explored the core concepts of this book, this section provides a comprehensive collection of over 500 practical, HR-approved phrases you can use to communicate effectively with coworkers. These suggested phrases have been conveniently organized into the following table by chapter to offer you easy access and serve as a quick reference guide.

THE HR-APPROVED WHAT-TO-SAY CHEATSHEET

INTRODUCTION

1. Yeah, because do you really need another email?

CHAPTER 1: COMMUNICATION & INTERPERSONAL CONFLICTS

2. Interruptions are like speed bumps on the road to productivity.
3. Your input is valuable, but let's ensure everyone has a chance to speak.

4. Can we take turns sharing ideas to make sure everyone feels heard?

5. I appreciate your enthusiasm, but let's pause to hear other perspectives.

6. Appreciate the cryptic approach—it adds a fun escape-room vibe! Mind giving me the decoder key so I can crack this one?

7. Your memos are becoming my favorite workplace mystery series—any hints for solving today's episode?

8. This memo reads like corporate poetry—can we do a quick analysis to make sure I'm not missing any metaphors?

9. Appreciate the creative briefing, but can we quickly translate this into plain English for clarity's sake?

10. Meetings without agendas are my favorite guessing games— any clues on today's plot?

11. Today's agenda is mysterious—care to shed some light?

12. Love surprises, but can we have an agenda teaser next time?

13. Meeting surprise parties are fun, but a little agenda spoiler would be nice.

14. Emails without subjects feel like surprise gifts—can we unwrap some context first?

15. Subject lines help me prioritize—mind including one next time?

16. Inbox detective work is thrilling—still, a subject line might save some guesswork.

17. Clear subject lines are like GPS for my inbox—can we set the coordinates next time?

18. Thanks for your feedback. It's like GPS for improvement!

19. Feedback is fuel for growth. Appreciate you filling my tank!

20. Your insights are helpful. Let's keep the feedback loop spinning.

21. Constructive feedback noted. Let's continue improving together.

22. I appreciate brevity, but your email left out the plot twist— care to elaborate?

23. Brief emails are great, but clarity is even better.

24. I love succinctness, but a few more details would help me understand your point.
25. Your email was intriguing—can you expand on that thought?
26. Miscommunications are puzzles—let's piece together a clear picture.
27. Looks like we have a communication gap—let's bridge it clearly.
28. Messages got mixed—can we clarify to ensure alignment?
29. Let's quickly clarify to ensure we're speaking the same language.
30. Your voicemail was intriguing but a bit cliffhanger-ish—can we get the full episode?
31. Brief voicemails are efficient, but clarity is key—could you elaborate?
32. I appreciate concise voicemails—mind adding a touch more detail next time?
33. Voicemail puzzle received—any chance of solving it together?
34. Silence in meetings feels mysterious—anyone want to break the ice?
35. Quiet meetings are serene, but I'd love to hear everyone's thoughts.
36. Let's avoid silent films—your voice matters!
37. Input from everyone keeps our team strong—feel free to jump in!
38. Appreciate your creative flair, but let's aim for straightforwardness in our communications.
39. Artistic expression is wonderful—let's also ensure clarity for the team.
40. Your approach is unique—mind adding a bit more clarity for universal understanding?
41. Creativity is valued—clarity is cherished.

CHAPTER 2: PERFORMANCE & RESPONSIBILITY ISSUES

42. Teamwork makes the dream work—but only if we're all dreaming the same dream.
43. Is this a solo performance, or can we aim for a team symphony?
44. Your solo skills are great, but teamwork takes us further.
45. Collaboration turns good ideas into great ones—let's collaborate more!
46. Appreciate your superhero speed, but let's align as a team first.
47. Solo sprints are impressive—but relay races win championships.
48. Going fast is exciting, but going together gets us farther.
49. Let's align our paces to cross the finish line together.
50. Did we just enter a competition, or can we aim for collaboration?
51. Competition can motivate, but collaboration builds lasting success.
52. Let's save competition for trivia night—today's about teamwork.
53. We win bigger when we win together.
54. Your delegation skills are impressive, but can we also discuss involvement?
55. Let's aim for balanced delegation—clear roles keep the team strong.
56. I appreciate delegation, but staying involved keeps us all informed.
57. Clearer delegation helps everyone succeed—let's clarify roles.
58. Invisible fences aren't great for teamwork—let's build visible bridges instead.
59. Boundaries matter, but let's ensure they don't become barriers.
60. Healthy boundaries support great teamwork—let's set them clearly.
61. Clarifying boundaries helps us avoid stepping on toes and keep productivity high.

62. Our project is getting adventurous—shall we set clearer paths?
63. Clear project guidelines help us stay on the same adventure.
64. Navigating without clear roles feels risky—let's chart the course together.
65. Clear roles ensure smooth sailing—let's define responsibilities.
66. Appreciate the initiative, but solo ventures can steer us off course.
67. Solo missions are risky—let's keep teamwork at the helm.
68. Let's double-check our coordinates to ensure we're all heading the same way.
69. Team alignment is our compass—let's recalibrate if needed.
70. Ideas love company—let's discuss them openly.
71. Sharing ideas boosts creativity—let's encourage more brainstorming sessions.
72. Feedback loops make our ideas stronger—let's keep them flowing.
73. Encouraging open dialogue helps everyone contribute effectively.
74. Communication is the glue of teamwork—let's keep it strong and sticky.
75. Let's ensure clarity in our team discussions to avoid misunderstandings.
76. Listening actively helps us align better—let's sharpen our ears.
77. Clear communication helps us move smoothly from plan to execution.
78. Appreciate your hustle, but teamwork needs synchronized rhythms.
79. Synchronized teamwork ensures our collective success.
80. Let's sync our watches—teamwork runs best on the same schedule.
81. Togetherness is our strength—let's nurture it daily.

CHAPTER 3: RESPECT & PERSONAL BOUNDARIES

82. Should I start charging rent for desk visits, or can we agree on some space boundaries?
83. Did we merge desks without me knowing?
84. Are you auditing my workspace, or is this just a friendly inspection?
85. I appreciate your suggestions, but I'd prefer more personal workspace to stay focused.
86. Our conversations are turning into duets—can I finish my solo first?
87. If interrupting were a sport, you'd be the champion.
88. Maybe we can save your comments for the director's cut version?
89. Let's find a system that allows everyone to finish their thoughts clearly.
90. Thanks, but I canceled my subscription to workplace gossip.
91. Sounds interesting, but my gossip meter is already maxed out.
92. My drama quota is full—got anything productivity-related?
93. I'd prefer if we kept conversations positive and work-focused.
94. Careful, HR might ask you to guest-star in their next training video.
95. Is this a comedy special, or should we tone it down?
96. Your jokes always spice things up—maybe keep the spice workplace-appropriate?
97. Let's aim for humor that's comfortable for everyone.
98. Looks like your message arrived after my work-life boundaries kicked in.
99. After-hours texts are against my phone's union rules.
100. Night-time emails require premium subscription—I'm only basic tier.
101. In the interest of balance, let's keep work discussions during regular hours.
102. Should I start charging admission fees, or can we agree to keep eyes on our own screens?
103. Want a tour of my screen, or just window-shopping?

104. Curious about my desktop decor, or genuinely needing something?

105. If you need something, just let me know directly—I'd appreciate more privacy.

106. My notifications clocked out early yesterday—catching up now!

107. My inbox sleeps early—let's handle it tomorrow.

108. Looks like your message arrived after my brain powered down.

109. To keep a healthy work-life balance, let's stick to communication during working hours.

110. Did my promotion take a scenic route, or should we talk about directions?

111. Looks like my job description is turning into a mystery novel—can we clarify the plot?

112. I think my contributions turned invisible again—mind helping me make them apparent?

113. Turns out my network is smaller than my Wi-Fi range—care to help me expand coverage?

114. My achievements keep entering a recognition black hole—should we launch a rescue mission?

115. Did my feedback go into spam, or are we just overdue for a chat?

116. My role description turned into a choose-your-own-adventure—mind helping pick the right chapter?

117. My accomplishments keep missing the awards ceremony—time for directions?

118. I'd appreciate discussing ways to ensure recognition aligns with contributions.

119. Looks like we've hit jargon turbulence—shall we decode these terms for clarity?

120. Guess my references just celebrated their retirement—any newer favorites to recommend?

121. My emoji seems to have gone rogue—sorry for the confusion!

122. Virtual backgrounds: keeping our laundry secrets since 2020.

CHAPTER 4: TOXIC BEHAVIOR & NEGATIVE
ATTITUDES

123. If pessimism were an Olympic sport, you'd be undefeated—but how about helping us score some positivity points?
124. Your inner critic deserves a vacation—let's book it a trip.
125. You're great at finding clouds—let's start looking for silver linings.
126. Constructive feedback is valuable—let's focus on solutions to improve outcomes.
127. Our office drama could win Daytime Emmys—but how about we save spoilers and stick to facts?
128. Your stories rival daytime TV—but maybe let's save drama for after-hours.
129. You're our in-house gossip columnist—maybe focus more on good news?
130. Let's keep conversations focused on factual information to avoid misunderstandings.
131. I didn't realize intimidation was on today's meeting agenda—let's try collaboration instead.
132. Your management style feels like boot camp—can we aim for team-building exercises instead?
133. Could we redirect that negativity toward finding a solution?
134. Your gloomy forecasts could use a dose of optimism—care to collaborate on that?
135. Appreciate your realism, but let's also highlight potential positives.
136. Constant criticism might boost toughness, but positivity fuels real progress.
137. Could we shift from blame games to solution brainstorming?
138. Your detective skills for faults are impeccable—now, let's detect solutions.
139. You have a knack for spotting problems—let's put that talent toward solving them.
140. We all appreciate honesty, but let's keep it constructive.

141. Appreciate your attention to detail—can we channel it positively?
142. Negativity is catchy—let's start an optimism trend instead.
143. Your sarcasm game is strong, but clarity and kindness might win more friends.
144. Let's aim for clarity without the sarcastic undertone.
145. If sarcasm had awards, you'd sweep—but let's aim for clarity instead.
146. Sarcasm is fun, but straightforwardness might get us further.
147. Cynicism is fascinating, but hopefulness gets things done.
148. Skepticism can be healthy, but optimism keeps us moving forward.
149. Your skepticism is insightful, but let's balance it with proactive steps.
150. Doubt is useful in moderation—let's also embrace possibilities.
151. Critiques are welcome—let's ensure they help build, not break.
152. I admire your critical eye—mind pairing it with some constructive suggestions?
153. Constructive critiques are far more valuable—let's focus on those.
154. Let's swap complaints for ideas—we'll all feel more productive.
155. Maybe complaints should come with a complimentary solution attached?
156. Constant negativity creates a tough climate—let's try to clear the air.
157. Our morale could use a positivity boost—care to lead the charge?
158. You've identified the problem clearly—how about we identify solutions just as clearly?
159. Problems without solutions are just hurdles—let's start jumping them.
160. Could we shift from dwelling on issues to actively solving them?

161. Your honesty is valuable—let's make sure it builds rather than bruises.
162. Maybe we could turn this complaint session into a strategy session?
163. Your critique is sharp—let's make it productive.

CHAPTER 5: ETHICS & PROFESSIONAL CONDUCT

164. Loved your presentation—probably because it sounded exactly like the notes I wrote last week. Maybe we can collaborate openly next time?
165. Impressive recall of my ideas—how about giving a co-author credit next time?
166. Great minds think alike, but let's clarify who thought first.
167. To keep teamwork transparent, I'd appreciate acknowledgment for my contributions.
168. It seems we're sharing a creative wavelength again—maybe next time, we should announce our ideas together?
169. Chapter 5: Ethics & Professional Conduct
170. Are you borrowing everyone's notes, or are we just creatively synced?
171. We might need to patent our joint ideas—want to co-present next time?
172. To maintain clarity and fairness, let's openly recognize everyone's input.
173. It looks like promotions require a secret handshake—mind teaching it to the rest of us?
174. Does the employee of the month title come with a membership card, or can anyone apply?
175. Your star performer might appreciate some company in the spotlight.
176. Clear criteria for opportunities would help keep morale high and team dynamics balanced.
177. I appreciate speed, but let's avoid the 'fix-it-later' method—it's getting a bit too thrilling.
178. Fast work is great, but accuracy deserves some love, too.

179. I admire your efficiency, but let's not give quality the day off.
180. Balancing speed and quality ensures we maintain our team's strong reputation.
181. Looks like our numbers took up creative writing—let's get back to nonfiction.
182. Financial fiction might be interesting reading, but let's stick to facts.
183. The books don't need a plot twist—accuracy is dramatic enough.
184. Integrity in our reporting is crucial for our credibility and success.
185. Your leaks are giving office gossip columns a run for their money—let's tighten things up.
186. Did your confidentiality clause go on vacation?
187. Your gossip scoop is too hot—maybe stick to cooler, less sensitive topics.
188. Maintaining confidentiality protects trust and ensures professionalism.
189. Your receipts are pretty magical lately—should we review the accounting rules before finance does its own magic trick?
190. Your expenses might win a creativity award, but accounting prefers facts.
191. Looks like you're pioneering expense reporting innovations —maybe check policy first?
192. Accuracy in reporting expenses helps maintain our team's integrity.
193. Missed you again today—should we start booking a hologram, or do you prefer traditional invites?
194. Your attendance is becoming legendary—how about joining us in person next time?
195. Should we send out a search party or just set extra reminders?
196. Your participation is valuable. Please prioritize attending future meetings.

CHAPTER 6: BOSS INTERACTIONS &
MICROMANAGEMENT

197. Thinking of pulling up a chair, or can we set regular check-ins instead?

198. Is today's viewing a special feature, or can I continue the regular programming?

199. Would you prefer a live feed, or should I send highlights later?

200. I appreciate your attention. Let's set up regular updates to streamline the process.

201. Loved your summary of my work—next time, can we co-present to make it official?

202. Impressive summary—next time, can we include the author's credits?

203. Your retelling of my ideas has great flair—how about we present jointly next time?

204. Loved your summary of my work–next time, for my growth and development, I would love to be involved to co-present and make it official?

205. I appreciate your enthusiasm for my ideas. Next time, let's collaborate on the presentation together.

206. Maybe it's time we cut the puppet strings—think I could audition for a solo act on the next project?

207. Should I rehearse my puppet act, or could I take a solo performance this round?

208. I promise I'll perform even better if you loosen the strings just a little.

209. Let's try giving me more autonomy. I'm confident it will improve my performance.

210. I think my accomplishments turned invisible again—mind if we spotlight them briefly?

211. Maybe my work achievements have turned invisible—can we check your visibility settings?

212. Did my accomplishments slip into stealth mode? Let me share them again clearly.

213. I'd appreciate discussing my recent achievements to ensure alignment and recognition.

214. I see my work inspired another round of commentary—any chance I could get a few spoiler alerts next time?

215. Your feedback keeps my ego humble, but solutions might boost my confidence even more.

216. You're a master of critique—care to also share the secret recipe for improvement?

217. Constructive feedback is always welcome. Let's identify specific ways I can improve.

218. I must've missed the auditions for favorite employee—mind sharing the application details?

219. Do I need a VIP membership for the good assignments, or is there a waiting list?

220. If there's a secret handshake for preferred status, count me in next time!

221. To ensure fairness, can we set clearer guidelines for assigning opportunities?

222. Our deadlines always have dramatic entrances—can we schedule them earlier to avoid the cliffhangers?

223. Deadlines don't need surprise parties—regular invites are just fine.

224. These last-minute requests feel like cliffhangers—can we try a less suspenseful approach?

225. Consistent scheduling helps everyone stay productive—let's plan deadlines earlier.

226. My notifications clocked out early yesterday—catching up now!

227. My inbox sleeps early—let's handle it tomorrow.

228. My inbox practices strict bedtime—even if I don't always follow suit.

229. Love chatting with you, but let's save work stuff for when we're both on the clock!

230. Our project goals seem to have commitment issues—maybe we can help them settle down this time?

231. These moving targets are giving me whiplash—let's anchor them down.

232. Are our project goals testing their freedom, or can we lock them down soon?

233. For smoother execution, let's agree on firm project objectives from the start.

CHAPTER 7: CAREER GROWTH & RECOGNITION

234. Looks like my promotion got lost in the mail—can we track it down together?

235. Did my promotion take a scenic route, or should we talk about directions?

236. Feels like I'm stuck in promotion traffic—any tips to clear the road?

237. I'd appreciate discussing specific steps I can take to improve and advance.

238. My job description feels like a mystery novel lately—can we clarify the plot?

239. My role description turned into a choose-your-own-adventure—mind helping pick the right chapter?

240. Seems my responsibilities became a bit adventurous—let's map them clearly.

241. I'd appreciate some clarity on my responsibilities to ensure I'm aligned with team goals.

242. I think my contributions turned invisible again—mind helping me make them apparent?

243. My latest ideas went stealth mode again—can we turn off invisibility settings?

244. Did my accomplishments activate ghost mode? Time for a quick spotlight?

245. I'd appreciate your advice on increasing visibility for my contributions.

246. Turns out my network is smaller than my Wi-Fi range—care to help me expand coverage?

247. I think my network is buffering—mind helping me refresh my connections?

248. My professional circle feels like dial-up internet—let's speed things up!

249. I'd value your guidance on expanding my internal network to grow professionally.

250. Looks like my achievements keep entering a recognition black hole—should we launch a rescue mission?

251. Did my achievements disappear into a recognition vortex again?

252. My accomplishments keep missing the awards ceremony—time for directions?

253. I'd appreciate discussing ways to ensure recognition aligns with contributions.

254. Feedback seems scarce lately—should I send out a search party or schedule a meeting?

255. Did my feedback go into spam, or are we just overdue for a chat?

256. My growth would appreciate regular check-ins, or do we need a treasure map?

257. I'd like to schedule regular feedback sessions to support my ongoing development.

258. My job description is starting to feel like a choose-your-own-adventure story—mind helping me pick the right page?

259. Feels like my role took a detour—can we get it back on the main road?

260. My tasks are getting creative—maybe too creative. Could we refocus?

261. I'd appreciate clarifying my job duties to ensure we're aligned on expectations.

262. I think my accomplishments fell into the office black hole again—any chance we could pull them back into orbit?

263. Did my recent wins turn invisible again? Let's try spotlighting them.

264. My achievements might need GPS—they keep missing your radar.

265. I'd appreciate feedback and recognition to help guide my ongoing efforts.

266. Feels like my career ladder is missing a few rungs—mind helping me rebuild it?
267. Is my career path under construction? Let's build a clear route.
268. My advancement feels like climbing stairs in the dark—care to shine a light?
269. Could we discuss actionable steps I can take to advance my career here?

CHAPTER 8: EMAIL & DIGITAL COMMUNICATION

270. Your subject line nearly triggered my emergency response system—can we agree to save all caps for genuine office emergencies?
271. My heart just survived your all-caps surprise—let's keep future emails lowercase.
272. Next time, let's save all-caps for actual fires or urgent pizza deliveries.
273. For clarity, could we reserve uppercase for truly urgent matters?
274. Oops, looks like my emoji got lost in translation—just kidding, no sarcasm intended!
275. My emoji seems to have gone rogue—sorry for the confusion!
276. Did my humor emoji malfunction again? Let me clarify.
277. I apologize if my message was unclear. Here's what I actually meant.
278. Just letting you know your message safely arrived, but my inbox is having a busy moment. I'll send a thoughtful reply by end of day!
279. Your email arrived just in time for my afternoon email marathon.
280. Email traffic jam on my side—clearing it shortly!
281. I've received your request and will respond fully by the end of the day.

282. Your sign-off threw me off balance—was it shorthand or just an accidental cliffhanger?
283. Your sign-off left me with a dramatic cliffhanger!
284. Your emails end faster than my internet connection on a bad day.
285. I wanted to check in briefly—your email seemed a bit abrupt; is everything okay?
286. Apologies for that informality slip—my brain briefly entered weekend mode!
287. Looks like my chat went into casual Friday mode—let me clarify.
288. My autocorrect chose informality toda. Here's a more professional take!
289. I apologize for my informal wording earlier. Here's a clearer response.
290. Sorry everyone, my inbox wanted some company and went rogue!
291. My inbox staged a "Reply All" rebellion—apologies for the digital chaos!
292. Sorry for triggering an inbox avalanche—the next "Reply All" requires my supervisor's approval.
293. Apologies for the extra messages. I'll be more careful moving forward.
294. Your messages are great brain teasers—any chance we can skip to clarity next time?
295. Are your messages a secret code? I forgot to bring my decoder ring today.
296. Should I call Sherlock to decode your latest note, or could we simplify things?
297. Clearer messages would help us stay aligned and productive —mind elaborating next time?
298. My phone's strict bedtime kept your message waiting— ready to respond now!
299. Late-night messages get put in the digital waiting room until morning.
300. My inbox clocks out earlier than I do—sorry for the delay!

301. To keep work-life balance healthy, let's handle non-urgent items during office hours.

302. Emails are stacking up faster than I can read—time for a strategy shift?

303. Is my inbox holding a message convention? Let's clear things out efficiently.

304. My inbox turned into a traffic jam—sorting it out ASAP!

305. Quick heads-up—your email was briefly caught in my spam net, responding now!

306. Your email enthusiasm is admirable—mind pacing replies so we all stay caught up?

307. Your reply speed is impressive. Let's ensure clarity matches pace!

308. Think of emails like fine dining—let's savor clear, concise messages rather than binge on lengthy ones.

309. Your CC list rivals my friends list on social media—can we narrow it down a bit?

310. Let's trim our CC list—less is definitely more effective!

311. CC overload detected—shall we streamline the audience for clarity?

312. Reducing CC clutter will help us focus clearly on the relevant recipients.

313. Attachments without context feel like surprise guests—let's introduce them properly next time.

314. Attachments arrived incognito—mind giving them proper introductions next time?

CHAPTER 9: MANAGING CROSS-GENERATIONAL HUMOR

315. Maybe my comedy references need updating—what's everyone binge-watching these days?

316. Note to self: save retro sitcom jokes for nostalgia night.

317. Looks like my humor has an expiration date—any fresher suggestions?

318. I'd love to hear everyone's favorite comedies to find common ground.
319. Sorry, I forgot memes don't come with subtitles—let me explain!
320. Memes should really come with age ratings—let me break this down.
321. Next time, I'll attach meme translations for easier viewing.
322. Let me provide context to ensure we're all on the same page.
323. Sarcasm alert—looks like we need an interpreter to translate Gen X humor.
324. Sarcasm just triggered an office-wide buffering moment—allow me to clarify.
325. Sarcasm detected! Initiating translation mode.
326. Let's briefly clarify to ensure everyone's comfortable and clear.
327. Comedy has certainly evolved—let's appreciate everyone's unique comedic styles!
328. Humor diversity check complete—everyone's style is welcome here.
329. Glad we covered comedy across the generations—who says we can't multitask?
330. Appreciating each other's humor helps strengthen our team's connection.
331. Irony alert! For anyone not fluent in Millennial humor, let's unpack that joke together.
332. Caution: irony detected—context loading in 3, 2, 1...
333. Your honesty just caused a generation-gap hiccup—let's smooth it out.
334. Let's clarify briefly to ensure everyone's comfortable and on board.
335. Your emoji-to-text ratio is record-breaking—any chance we could have fewer pictures and more subtitles next time?
336. Emoji literacy course now open for enrollment.
337. My emoji fluency isn't great—mind throwing in some actual words?

338. Clearer messaging can ensure everyone understands your intended meaning.
339. Looks like we've hit jargon turbulence—shall we decode these terms for clarity?
340. Corporate-speak translation service activated—decoding in progress.
341. Let's dust off the jargon dictionary to keep everyone on track.
342. Clear terminology helps everyone follow the discussion effectively.
343. Guess my references just celebrated their retirement—any newer favorites to recommend?
344. Did my movie references go vintage overnight, or am I just classic now?
345. My pop-culture database needs an update—mind sharing your latest favorites?
346. Let's find some common cultural references to connect everyone comfortably.
347. My analogies might be too analog for this digital age—open to updates!
348. Sorry if my joke felt outdated—let's find humor that resonates with everyone.
349. Pop culture quiz failed—time for a refresher!
350. Can we agree to translate generational slang to keep everyone included?
351. Your abbreviations triggered my Google search—mind providing translations?
352. Acronyms should come with subtitles—let's spell things out clearly.
353. Let's navigate generational differences by clarifying jargon and slang openly.
354. Who knew jokes had an expiration date? Let's keep the humor fresh.
355. Did humor just skip a generation? Let's bridge the gap!
356. Lost in humor translation—mind breaking down that reference?

357. Clarifying our cultural references can ensure everyone feels included.

CHAPTER 10: CHANGE MANAGEMENT &
ADDRESSING VOLATILITY

358. Looks like the tech gods decided we needed a surprise challenge—time for a team training montage!
359. The software fairy dropped another update—let's decode it together.
360. Who knew our keyboards would need survival training this week?
361. Let's schedule a training session to ensure everyone feels confident about the new software.
362. Welcome to our new corporate reality show—let's skip the drama and go straight to Q&A.
363. Our merger is like a surprise guest—let's make sure everyone gets acquainted.
364. Is it merger season already? Let's clear the air and get aligned.
365. Regular discussions will help everyone navigate the merger clearly and confidently.
366. We might be remote, but awkward team-building exercises can still follow us home!
367. Welcome to our pajama-friendly work zone—let's keep connected!
368. Time to perfect our video-call smiles—daily check-ins start today.
369. Regular virtual meetings will keep our teamwork strong and connected.
370. Looks like we're playing musical chairs in leadership—let's sit tight and keep dancing.
371. Our leadership carousel spins again—let's ensure we all stay steady.
372. Another round of executive musical chairs—grab a seat and let's strategize.

373. Transparent communication will keep everyone informed during this transition.
374. Policy update incoming—brace yourselves for some exciting reading material! Let's decode it together.
375. Policies got an unexpected reboot—let's unpack them calmly.
376. Surprise: policy makeover! Let's navigate these changes together.
377. Training sessions on new policies will ensure everyone adapts comfortably and clearly.
378. Looks like it's time for a team reboot—how about we support each other through this update?
379. Did someone install a revolving door? Let's stabilize things together.
380. Looks like turnover season again—let's strengthen our team bonds.
381. Mentorship programs will help everyone feel supported during transitions.
382. Office relocation adventure ahead! Pack your coffee mugs and your sense of humor—we're on the move.
383. Looks like our desks are taking a field trip—let's pack smartly.
384. Change of scenery incoming! Who's ready for a fresh view?
385. Clear communication about the move timeline will help everyone adjust smoothly.
386. Hold onto your lanyards—we're boarding the rebranding rollercoaster. Let's clarify what this means together.
387. Our brand just got a makeover—time for a guided tour!
388. Brand facelift incoming—let's figure out our new look together.
389. Clear explanations about brand changes will keep the team informed and aligned.
390. Welcome to 'Who's Who in the New Crew'—let's clear up the cast list!
391. Role shuffle season—let's get everyone on the same page.

392. Did our job titles just do a dance routine? Time to learn the new choreography.

393. Regular check-ins will clarify roles and help the team stay cohesive.

CHAPTER 11: WORKPLACE ENVIRONMENT & PRODUCTIVITY

394. My ergonomic chair asked me nicely to tidy its surroundings —it's feeling lonely in all this clutter.

395. Turns out my ergonomic chair prefers zen minimalism—time for a desk makeover.

396. My desk chaos has reached legendary status—let's write a tidy sequel.

397. Organizing my workspace will significantly enhance my productivity and clarity.

398. Office noise levels are hitting rock concert status—headphones, here I come!

399. Found my productivity secret weapon—white noise playlist activated.

400. Noise-canceling headphones have helped me concentrate better in our active workspace.

401. Social media quarantine mode activated—time to get serious.

402. Temporarily muting distractions—catch up with you when I resurface.

403. I'm creating distraction-free zones during work hours to boost productivity.

404. Time to rescue my desk from creative chaos—it's begging for some organization therapy.

405. Desk art installation reaching critical mass—decluttering intervention needed.

406. My sticky-note collection needs a digital upgrade—time to organize!

407. Maintaining an organized workspace helps me stay creative and productive.

408. My computer decided it prefers retirement to upgrades—mind helping me negotiate a tech refresh?
409. My computer wants to retire early—can we discuss an upgrade?
410. Think my tech joined the slow-lane club—time for an intervention?
411. Upgrading our equipment will significantly enhance my ability to deliver effectively.
412. Our thermostat has more drama than reality TV—can we negotiate a peace treaty?
413. Temperature wars escalating again—time to call for a peace summit.
414. Thermostat negotiations ongoing—let's aim for a temperature UN Assembly.
415. Establishing a comfortable office temperature will help everyone work productively. Let's research what the average office temperature normally is and agree.
416. The breakroom mess is gaining historical status—let's not make future archeologists guess our habits.
417. The kitchen sink is resembling abstract art—let's aim for realism.
418. Breakroom mysteries solved: dishes don't clean themselves.
419. Maintaining cleanliness in common areas keeps the workplace pleasant for everyone.
420. Introducing 'Room Wars'—may the scheduling odds be in your favor!
421. Welcome to the great conference room reservation rally—please, play nicely!
422. Conference Room Chronicles—let the scheduling games begin!
423. A shared booking system helps ensure fair and efficient use of our meeting spaces. Let's get a system in place that we all follow.
424. Looks like our desks are taking a field trip—let's pack smartly.
425. Change of scenery incoming! Who's ready for a fresh view?

426. Clear communication about the move timeline will help everyone adjust smoothly.
427. Your complaint skills are unmatched. Ready to switch sides and champion solutions?
428. Maybe complaints should come with a complimentary solution attached?
429. Let's address issues constructively by suggesting improvements and solutions.
430. Fast work is great, but accuracy deserves some love, too.
431. I admire your efficiency, but let's not give quality the day off.
432. Balancing speed and quality ensures we maintain our team's strong reputation.

CHAPTER 12: CONFLICT RESOLUTION & DIFFICULT CONVERSATIONS

433. Is this a debate club, or can we aim for consensus-building instead?
434. Let's shift from courtroom drama to collaborative problem-solving.
435. Feels like we've hit a conversational roadblock—can we reroute towards solutions?
436. Constructive conversations lead to actionable solutions—let's aim for clarity.
437. I appreciate your passion—how about we channel it into problem-solving?
438. Your enthusiasm is great, but let's make sure it helps us move forward.
439. Can we transform this passion into a proactive solution?
440. Let's turn disagreement into dialogue for a more productive conversation.
441. Conflict is natural, but solutions are even better—let's find some.
442. Finding common ground will help us resolve this effectively.
443. Our conversation hit turbulence—let's steady the flight path toward understanding.

444. Let's approach this calmly to ensure mutual respect and clear communication.
445. Resolving this amicably will help us both move forward positively.
446. Could we schedule a dedicated time to discuss this thoroughly and respectfully?
447. Let's aim for win-win outcomes to keep our teamwork strong.
448. Let's keep the conversation constructive to find the best solution together.
449. This discussion feels heated—let's take a moment to cool down and revisit.
450. We seem stuck—let's take a step back and reassess calmly.
451. Let's pause, reflect, and reconvene when we've all cooled off.
452. I sense frustration—maybe we could briefly step away and then return refreshed?
453. Are we on a reality show? Let's keep our drama productive and solution-focused.
454. Your points are strong, but can we deliver them with a bit less drama?
455. If this was a TV show, ratings would be high—but let's focus on solutions instead.
456. Let's maintain professionalism even when we strongly disagree.
457. Let's clarify misunderstandings before they escalate.
458. I think we might be misunderstanding each other—let's clarify things first.
459. Before we go further, let's ensure we understand each other clearly.
460. Could we briefly summarize to ensure we're all aligned?
461. I hear what you're saying, but let's ensure it translates into clear, actionable steps.
462. Miscommunication can derail us—let's confirm our understanding clearly.
463. Let's ensure clarity, so we're all aligned moving forward.
464. We're better together—let's find a common path forward.

465. Let's avoid escalating conflict and find cooperative strategies instead.
466. I appreciate your honesty—can we use it to build trust and solutions?
467. Transparency helps us grow—let's aim for open and respectful dialogue.
468. We can disagree respectfully and still move forward constructively.
469. Your perspective is valuable—let's integrate it positively.
470. To resolve this effectively, let's actively listen and clarify each other's points.
471. Communication is key—let's unlock solutions together.
472. Finding solutions together strengthens our team's bonds.
473. Let's find a path forward that respects everyone's viewpoint.

QUIZ RESULTS

474. Appreciate the creative briefing, but could we quickly translate this into plain English for clarity's sake?
475. Looks like we have a lot of perspectives—I vote for less inbox ping-pong and a quick video huddle to align.
476. Your comment landed differently than I think you intended. Can we briefly unpack it together?
477. We've got competing priorities doing their best impressions of emergencies. Shall we sort them calmly together?
478. We might have accidentally invented a new language between us. Shall we decode it together?
479. Your deadlines seem to enjoy scenic detours—want help creating a roadmap to the finish line?
480. We need a tool that helps ensure credit and blame get distributed equally—it's democracy, workplace-style!
481. Your disappearing acts are impressive—but we need your starring role for the whole show.
482. Looks like this task is giving you a tough time—want to tag-team it or call in backup?

483. Your drafts have great suspense—I never know which errors I'll find next! Want help making it less thrilling for everyone?

484. Should I start charging rent for desk visits, or can we agree on some space boundaries?

485. Our conversations are turning into duets—can I finish my solo first?

486. Thanks, but I canceled my subscription to workplace gossip.

487. Careful, HR might ask you to guest-star in their next training video.

488. Looks like your message arrived after my work-life boundaries kicked in.

489. If pessimism were an Olympic sport, you'd be undefeated— can you help us score some positivity points?

490. Our office drama could win Daytime Emmys— how about we save spoilers and stick to facts?

491. I didn't realize intimidation was on today's meeting agenda —let's try collaboration instead.

492. I admire your skill in compliments—you always keep us guessing. Mind giving your critique straight next time?

493. Your complaint skills are unmatched. Ready to switch sides and champion solutions so we can experience what you have in mind?

494. Seems there might be a VIP list for special assignments—any chance we could make the criteria public, so everyone gets a shot?

495. Looks like our numbers took up creative writing—let's get back to nonfiction.

496. Thinking of pulling up a chair, or can we set regular check-ins instead?

497. Maybe it's time we cut the puppet strings—think I could audition for a solo act on the next project?

498. Our project goals seem to have commitment issues—how can we help them settle down this time?

499. Your subject line nearly triggered my emergency response system—can we agree to save all caps for genuine office emergencies?

500. Oops, looks like my emoji got lost in translation—just kidding, no sarcasm intended!

501. Just letting you know your message safely arrived—but my inbox is having a busy moment. I'll send a thoughtful reply by end of day!

502. Your sign-off threw me off balance—was it shorthand or just an accidental cliffhanger?

503. Apologies for that informality slip—my brain briefly entered weekend mode!

504. Maybe my comedy references need updating—what's everyone binge-watching these days?

505. Sarcasm alert—looks like we need an interpreter to translate Gen-to-Gen humor.

506. Comedy has certainly evolved—let's appreciate everyone's unique comedic styles!

507. Your emoji-to-text ratio is record-breaking—any chance we could have fewer pictures and more subtitles next time?

508. Looks like the tech gods decided we needed a surprise challenge—time for a team training montage!

509. Welcome to our new corporate reality show—let's skip the drama and go straight to Q&A.

510. We might be remote, but awkward team-building exercises can still follow us home!

511. Looks like we're playing musical chairs in leadership—let's sit tight and keep dancing.

512. Policy update incoming—brace yourselves for some exciting reading material! Let's decode it together.

513. Office noise levels are hitting rock concert status—headphones, here I come!

514. Activating 'do not disturb' mode to avoid getting trapped in the social media abyss—see you on the other side!

515. My computer decided it prefers retirement to upgrades—mind helping me negotiate a tech refresh?

516. Our thermostat has more drama than reality TV—can we negotiate a peace treaty?

517. I've officially upgraded my work routine to tomatoes—productivity just got juicy!

518. Family hotline closed for business hours—normal service resumes after 5 PM.

519. These time zones have me feeling like a confused time traveler—someone passes the coffee and reminds me what year it is!

REFERENCES

Alleo. (2024, December 17). 7 Fun Productivity Game Strategies for Remote Workers to Balance Work and Play. Alleo. https://alleo.ai/blog/remote-workers/time-management/strategies-for-remote-workers-balancing-work-and-play-with-productivity-games/

Baynton, M. A., Crawford, L., Dr Samra, J., Workplace Strategies team. (2024, March 28). Setting Healthy Boundaries at Work. Workplace Strategies for Mental Health. https://www.workplacestrategiesformentalhealth.com/resources/setting-healthy-boundaries-at-work

Benz, J. (2019, July 9). How to Prevent and Address Bullying in the Workplace. Score. https://www.score.org/resource/blog-post/how-prevent-and-address-bullying-workplace

Berkeley Haas School of Business, Center for Equity, Gender and Leadership. (n.d.). Effective Communication in the Workplace. https://executive.berkeley.edu/thought-leadership/blog/effective-communication-workplace

Carucci, R. (2020, November 24). How to Actually Encourage Employee Accountability. Harvard Business Review. https://hbr.org/2020/11/how-to-actually-encourage-employee-accountability

Chiles, M. (2019, April 3). Viewpoint: How to Use Humor to Increase Employee Engagement. The Society for Human Resource

Management. https://www.shrm.org/topics-tools/news/employee-relations/viewpoint-how-to-use-humor-to-increase-employee-engagement

Chupradit, S., Haffar, M., Nassani, A. A., Yen Ku, K., & Zhenjing, G. (2022, May 13). Impact of Employees' Workplace Environment on Employees' Performance: A Multi-Mediation Model. Frontiers in Public Health. https://pmc.ncbi.nlm.nih.gov/articles/PMC9136218/

Criminal Watch Dog. (n.d.). Why You Need to Set Boundaries at Work & How to Do It. Criminal Watch Dog. https://www.criminal watchdog.com/resources/skill-development/setting-boundaries-at-work/

Cundall, M. (2017, November 11). HR Folks! Don't Worry Overmuch About Humor in the Workplace. LinkedIn. https://www.linkedin.com/pulse/hr-folks-dont-worry-overmuch-humor-workplace-michael-cundall

Dill-Ag13. (2024, April 24). Funny Project Management Sayings - Anyone Have a Printout? Reddit. https://www.reddit.com/r/project management/comments/1cby6jl/funny_project_management_say ings_anyone_have_a/

Doyle, A. M. (2023, June 2). Time Management Skills: Definition and Examples. The Balance Careers. https://www.thebalancemoney.com/time-management-skills-2063768

Examples.com. (n.d.). Examples of Sarcasm. Examples.com. https://www.examples.com/english/sarcasm-examples.html

Fishman Cohen, C. (n.d.). The Funny Side of Remote Working. iRelaunch. https://www.irelaunch.com/blog/the-funny-side-of-remote-working

Gallo, A. (2014, June 24). How to Help an Underperformer. Harvard Business School. https://hbr.org/2014/06/how-to-help-an-underperformer

Grammarly. (n.d.). Clarity in Writing: Definition, Examples, & Tips. Grammarly. https://www.grammarly.com/blog/clarity-in-writing/

Havens, J. (n.d.). 6 Hilarious Ethical Quandaries for Ethics Awareness Month. Jeff Havens. https://www.jeffhavens.com/news-and-updates/6-hilarious-ethical-quandaries-for-ethics-awareness-month

Huff, T. (2024, January 31). Laughing Across the Ages: Embracing

Generational Humor in the Workplace. Turknett Leadership Group. https://www.turknett.com/blog/embracing-generational-humor-in-the-workplace/

Human Resources. (2023, August 21). Navigating Workplace Humor: An HR Perspective. Exact Payroll. https://blog.exactpayroll.com/news/navigating-workplace-humor-an-hr-perspective

Indeed Editorial Team. (2025, March 4). 15 Examples of How To Increase Productivity in the Workplace. Indeed. https://www.indeed.com/career-advice/career-development/productivity

Indeed Editorial Team. (2025, January 29). 85 Funny Work Quotes to Share with Your Colleagues. Indeed. https://www.indeed.com/career-advice/career-development/funny-work-quotes

Indeed Editorial Team. (2023, February 22). Halo effect: Definition, Causes and Examples. Indeed Career Guide. https://www.indeed.com/career-advice/career-development/halo-effect

Indeed Editorial Team. (2025, January 29). How to Identify and Manage Toxic Coworkers (with Tips). Indeed Career Guide. https://www.indeed.com/career-advice/career-development/how-to-identify-and-manage-toxic-coworkers

Iwata, D., Jones, H., Martin, K., & Young-Havens, A. (2016, October). Los Angeles Community College District. https://www.laccd.edu/sites/laccd.edu/files/2022-09/10.16%20How%20to%20Effectively%20Communicate%20with%20Your%20Supervisor%20-%20Employee.pdf

Kerr, M. (2021, July 22). Create a Fun Video/Zoom Meetings Etiquette Guide. Mike Kerr. https://mikekerr.com/create-a-fun-video-zoom-meetings-etiquette-guide/

Knight, R. (2024, June 18). When Your New Boss Is a Micromanager. Harvard Business Review. https://hbr.org/2024/06/when-your-new-boss-is-a-micromanager

Li, A. (2025, January 7). How to Deal With Lack of Recognition and Appreciation at Work. Jobsolv. https://www.jobsolv.com/blog/how-to-deal-with-lack-of-recognition-and-appreciation-at-work

Luft, J., & Ingham, H. (1955). The Johari Window, a Graphic Model of Interpersonal Awareness. Proceedings of the Western Training Laboratory in Group Development.

Maurer, R. (2025, January 2). Managing Multi-Generational Communication in the Workplace. The Society for Human Resource Management. https://www.shrm.org/topics-tools/flagships/all-things-work/managing-multi-generational-communication-work place#:~:text=For%20example%2C%20research%20shows% 20that,in%20shorter%2C%20more%20casual%20bursts

Meritt Business Solutions. (n.d.). 8 Tips on Minimizing and Addressing Workplace Negativity. Meritt Business Solutions. https:// merrittbusiness.solutions/employee-experience/8-tips-on-minimiz ing-and-addressing-workplace-negativity/

Pollack, J. (2024, July 16). Managing Email-Based Conflicts. Pollack Peacebuilding Systems. https://pollackpeacebuilding.com/blog/ managing-email-based-conflicts/

Qualee. (n.d.). 15 Funny and Creative Employee Recognition and Awards Your Employees Will Love. Qualee. https://www.qualee. com/blog/funny-and-creative-employee-recognition-and-awards-your-employees-will-love

Quora. (n.d.). How Do You Use Sarcasm in Professional Settings Without Damaging Your Credibility? Quora. https://www.quora. com/How-do-you-use-sarcasm-in-professional-settings-without-damaging-your-credibility

Robinson, C. (2025, March 9). Laughter In Leadership: How Humor Enhances Workplace Performance. Forbes. https://www.forbes.com/ sites/cherylrobinson/2025/03/09/laughter-in-leadership-how-humor-enhances-workplace-performance/

Rowell, D., & Zucker, R. (2021, April 26). 6 Strategies for Leading Through Uncertainty. Harvard Business Journal. https://hbr.org/ 2021/04/6-strategies-for-leading-through-uncertainty

Smollan, R. (2020, November 10). Managing Stressful Organiza-tional Change. Psychology Today. https://www.psychologytoday. com/us/blog/stress-at-work/202011/managing-stressful-organiza tional-change

Somanathan, S. (2025, January 3). 50 Funny HR Jokes to Lighten the Mood at Work. ClickUp. https://clickup.com/blog/hr-jokes/

Sparkhall, H. (2022, November 8). "Humour, Seriously." I Was Terrified to Crack a Joke at Work Until I Read This Book. Medium.

https://medium.com/@HilarySparkhall123/humour-seriously-i-was-terrified-to-crack-a-joke-at-work-until-i-read-this-book-730305450b1a

Suarez, T. (n.d.). 20 Email Expressions to Ask for Clarification. Tannia Suarez. https://tanniasuarez.com/blog/clarification-email-expressions

Tipton, T. (2024, April 15). Change Management for Human Resources Professionals. Prosci. https://www.prosci.com/blog/hr-change-management-resources

Van Der Linden, L. (2023, October 12). 8 Steps to Effectively Handle Workplace Conflict. Forbes. https://www.forbes.com/sites/liesbethvanderlinden/2023/10/12/8-steps-to-effectively-handle-workplace-conflict/

Waldman, E. (2021, September 1). How to Manage a Multi-Generational Team. Harvard Business Journal. https://hbr.org/2021/08/how-to-manage-a-multi-generational-team

Webdev. (2024, January 2). Managing Disrespectful Employees. Front Line Leadership. https://frontlineleadershipprogram.com/managing-disrespectful-employees/

White, R. (2024, June 26). Funny Emails: 10 Examples of Hilarious Communication. Omnisend. https://www.omnisend.com/blog/funny-email-examples/

Wilkie, D. (2023, December 6). Workplace Gossip: What Crosses the Line? The Society for Human Resource Management. https://www.shrm.org/topics-tools/news/employee-relations/workplace-gossip-crosses-line